God's Signature Over the Nation's Capital:

Evidence of Your Christian Heritage

by Catherine Millard

SonRise Publications
New Wilmington, Pennsylvania

Dedication

To the United States of America, a country which opened its arms wide to me in my hour of need, and where I found the Pearl of Great Price — The Lord Jesus Christ.

Scripture quotations taken from the *New American Standard Bible,* copyright 1985 Holman Bible Publishers.

Copyright © 1985, 1988 by **Catherine Millard**

ISBN 0-936369-17-5
Library of Congress Catalogue Number: 88-060409

Photographer: **John W. Wrigley**
Illustrator: **Helen Weir**
Graphic Arts Advisor: **Maxwell Edgar**

Grateful acknowledgements:
To **Mrs. Florian Thayn,** Head of Art and Reference, Office of the Architect of the Capitol, for her invaluable assistance and encouragement during the many years of study and research in formulating this book from original sources.

To **Allison Heckler,** my first guide, whose cheerfulness, joy and love of the Lord was a constant source of inspiration to me during the early beginnings of this ministry.

Distributed by **Christian Heritage Tours, Inc.**

Published by **SonRise Publications**
Rt. 3, Box 202 New Wilmington, PA 16142

Graphic design and typography by **Publications Technologies**
Printed in the United States of America

4

Foreword

As a young student in France, I became fascinated with the heroes of America's founding period. Years later, after becoming an American citizen and a born-again Christian, I discovered that the source and strength of the noble ideals, values and characteristics of the founding fathers, was their Biblical faith.

It's an exciting study, so let us explore together our rich heritage, etched in marble and stone and woven into the very warp and woof of America's culture —through the architectural, artistic and historical themes inherent within and without her national landmarks, monuments and memorials.

Definitions

of terms used frequently in the text

Symbol—Something that stands for, or represents another thing; especially an object used to represent something abstract; an emblem; as, the dove is a symbol of peace, the cross is the symbol of Christianity.

Landmark—An event considered a high point or turning point of a period.

Monument—Something set up to keep alive the memory of a person or event, as a tablet, statue, pillar, building, etc.; a writing or the like serving as a memorial; a work, production, etc., of enduring value or significance; as, monuments of learning; vb ... to erect a monument to the memory of; as to monument a noble deed.

Memorial—Anything meant to help people remember some person or event, as a statue, holiday, etc. (e.g. Exodus 3:15; 17:14; Joshua 4:7; Acts of the Apostles 10:4)

Aesthetics—The theory of the fine arts and of people's responses to them; the science or that branch of philosophy which deals with the beautiful; the doctrines of taste.

(Webster's New 20th Century Dictionary — Unabridged — Second Edition)

Scripture parallels for the term "Memorial" added

6

Contents

Tour Stops

(Listed here in alphabetical order)

9

Freer Gallery of Art — 113
12th Street and Jefferson Davis Drive, S.W. on the Mall, Open 10 a.m. - 5:30 p.m. daily except Christmas Day; Tourmobile, Metro, bus or car.

Hirshhorn Museum & Sculpture Garden — 115
On the Mall & 8th St., S.W.; 10 a.m.-5:30 p.m. daily except Christmas. Longer hours during summer months; Tourmobile, Metro, bus or car.

Isabel la Catolica (the Statue of) — 150
In front of the Organization of American States, 17th and Constitution Avenue, N.W; Open 24 hours daily; Tourmobile, Metro, bus or car.

Jefferson Memorial — 20
Tidal Basin South Shore, West Potomac Park; 8 a.m.-midnight daily, except Christmas; Tourmobile, Metro, bus or car.

Kennedy Center for the Performing Arts — 139
Rock Creek Parkway at New Hampshire Ave. and F St., N.W; 10 a.m. to late evening daily; Tourmobile, Metro, bus or car.

Lafayette Square — 93
Between Pennsylvania Avenue and H Street, N.W., directly opposite the White House; Open 24 hours daily; Tourmobile, Metro, bus or car.

Library of Congress — 52
Capitol Hill, 1st St. and Independence Ave., S.E; Open 8:30 a.m.-9:30 p.m. Mon.- Fri; 8:30 a.m.- 5 p.m. Sat. and 1 p.m.- 5 p.m. Sun; Exhibit areas open until 6 p.m. Sat. and Sun; Closed Christmas and New Year's Day.

Lincoln Memorial — 155
West end of Mall — on line with 23rd Street, N.W; Open 8 a.m.-midnight, except Christmas; Tourmobile, Metro, bus or car.

Martin Luther (the Statue of) — 152
Thomas Circle, Massachusetts Avenue and 14th Street, N.W; Open 24 hours daily; Tourmobile, Metro, bus or car.

Metropolitan African Episcopal Methodist Church — 76
1518 M Street, N.W; Call for hours; Metro, bus or car

Metropolitan Memorial Methodist Church — 73
Nebraska and New Mexico Avenue, N.W; Call for hours; Bus or car.

National Air and Space Museum — 116
The Mall and 4th Street, S.W; Open 10 a.m.- 5:30 p.m. every day,except Christmas; Longer hours in the summer.

National Archives — 17
Constitution Ave. between 7th and 9th Sts., N.W; Open 10 a.m.-5:30 p.m. daily; Extended summer hours; Tourmobile, Metro, bus or car.

National Cathedral — 57
Mt. St. Alban, Wisconsin & Mass. Aves., 10 a.m.-4:30 p.m. Daily. Chapel of the Good Shepherd,24 hrs. Extended summer hours. Metro & bus; Bus, car

The Voice of America — 147
330 Independence Avenue, S.W; 30 min. guided tours: 8:45, 9:45, 10:45 a.m.; 1:45 and 2:45 p.m; Mon.- Fri; Tourmobile, Metro, bus or car.

Washington Cathedral *(see National Cathedral)* — 57

Washington Monument — 23
Center of Mall, Constitution Avenue at 15th St., N.W; Open 8 a.m. to midnight, April 1-Labor Day; 9 a.m.- 5 p.m. every day remainder of year except Christmas; Tourmobile, Metro, bus or car.

John Wesley (the Statue of) — 152
4400 Massachusetts Avenue, N.W., 24 hours; Bus or car.

White House — 29
1600 Pennsylvania Ave., N.W; Open 10 a.m.- Noon, Tues.-Sat; Closed Sun. and Mon; Tourmobile, Metro, bus or car.

John Witherspoon (the Statue of) — 152
17th and N Sts., N.W; 24 hours daily; Metro, bus or car.

VIRGINIA LOCATIONS

Arlington National Cemetery — 157
(Kennedy graves, Tomb of the Unknown Soldier); Directly west of Memorial Bridge in Arlington, Virginia; Open Oct. 1-March 31, 8 a.m.- 5 p.m; April 1-Sept. 30, 8 a.m.- 7 p.m; Changing of the guard — Winter, every hour on the hour; Summer—every half hour.

Christ Church — 91
Cameron and Columbus Sts. in Alexandria, Va.; Open 9 a.m.- 4 p.m. Mon.- Sat., 2 p.m.- 4 p.m. Sun., Nov. 1 -April 30; 9 a.m.-5 p.m. Mon.- Sat.; 2 p.m.- 4 p.m. Sun.-May 1 -Oct. 31; Metro and bus, bus or car.

Iwo Jima Memorial — 159
Virginia side of Memorial Bridge, between main entrance to Arlington Cemetery & Arlington Blvd. (U.S. 50); 24 hours; Metro, bus or car.

Mount Vernon, Virginia — 101
16 miles south of Washington on the George Washington Memorial Parkway; 9 a.m.- 4 p.m. Nov. 1-Feb. 28; 9 a.m.- 5 p.m. Mar. 1-Oct. 31; Tourmobile; bus or car.

Old Presbyterian Meeting House — 99
321 South Fairfax Street, Alexandria, Virginia; Call for hours; Metro and bus, bus or car.

Introduction

In speaking about the Constitution of the United States, several U.S. presidents have traced its effectiveness and solidity to the hand of Almighty God. In his Farewell Address to the nation delivered in 1796, George Washington, our first president, spoke about its value in these terms:

> "May Heaven continue to you the choicest tokens of its beneficence: that your union and brotherly affection may be perpetual: that the free Constitution, which is the work of your hands, may be sacredly maintained; that its administration in every department may be stamped with wisdom and virtue; that, in fine, the happiness of the people of these states, under the auspices of liberty, may be made complete by so careful a preservation and so prudent a use of this blessing as will acquire them the glory of recommending it to the applause, the affection and adoption of every nation which is yet a stranger to it ... It is of infinite moment that you should properly estimate the immense value of your national union to your collective and individual happiness; ... The name American, which belongs to you in your national capacity, must always exult the just pride of patriotism more than any appellation derived from local discriminations."

William Henry Harrison, ninth U.S. president, stated:

> "It is union that we want, not of a party for the sake of that party, but a union of the whole country, for the sake of the whole country, for the defense of its interests and its honor against foreign aggression, for the defense of those principles for which our ancestors so gloriously contended."

13

John Tyler, our tenth president, stated:

"Our prayers should evermore be offered up to the Father of the Universe for His wisdom to direct us in the path of our duty so as to enable us to consummate these high purposes."

Franklin Pierce, 14th president, boldly proclaimed:

"It is with me an earnest and vital belief that as the Union has been the source, under Providence, of our prosperity to this time, so it is the surest pledge of a continuance of the blessing we have enjoyed, which we are sacredly bound to transmit undiminished to our children."

Andrew Johnson, 17th U.S. president, stood upon the conviction that:

"The hand of Divine Providence was never more plainly visible in the affairs of the men than in the framing and adopting of the Constitution."

Our 18th president, Gen. Ulysses S. Grant, prayed for the nation as follows:

"I ask patient forbearance one toward another throughout the land, and a determined effort on the part of every citizen to do his share toward cementing a happy union, and I ask the prayers of the nation to Almighty God in behalf of this consummation."

The 23rd president, Benjamin Harrison, concluded:

"God has placed upon our head a diadem and has laid at our feet power and wealth beyond definition or calculation. But we must not forget that we take these gifts upon the condition that justice and mercy shall hold the reins of power and that the upward avenues of hope shall be free to all people."

Theodore Roosevelt, 26th president, shed further light on the heritage which is now ours to enjoy:

"But we have faith that we shall not prove false to the memories of the men of the mighty past. They did their work, they left us the splendid heritage we now enjoy. We in our turn have an assured confidence that we shall be able to leave this heritage unwasted and enlarged to our children's children."

While studying the origins and historical development of this great nation, it has been an amazing discovery to find that all current literature, including textbooks, history books, guidebooks and brochures pertaining to our blessed country have been robbed of their accuracy. Let me explain. In the earliest documentation we have on record at the Library of Congress of the United States, up through approximately 50 to 60 years ago, Christianity is woven into the warp and woof of this nation's history. The framers of the Constitution turned to

Scripture and prayer for guidance in formulating a new system of government, while most of America's greatest leaders, statesmen and inventors gave all glory to Almighty God, as the source and strength of their power and ability.

The need for this book is urgent, as we are

now evidencing the removal of tangible items of our precious American Christian heritage from national landmarks, monuments, memorials and shrines where the hand of God in the affairs of this nation is so boldly proclaimed.

The function and purpose of this book is therefore to take you by the hand through twelve fascinating tours at the seat of government, tracing America's rich Christian heritage as evidenced in the art, architecture, sculpture, inscriptions and historical memorabilia of the capital city of this nation under God.

Let us begin at the beginning:

In 1608 the area which now boasts of the nation's capital, and one of the world's greatest power centers, was discovered by Captain John Smith. George Washington chose this site himself in 1790 for the new federal city. At that time it lay mid-way between the northernmost and southernmost states. A year later, Washington appointed a French engineer by the name of Pierre Charles l'Enfant, who had served under him in the Revolutionary War, to draw up a plan for the new city. This imaginative, avant-garde designer mapped out the streets in a simple but practical manner. From the Capitol, he numbered the streets running north to south, lettering those which ran from east to west. Broad avenues, bearing the names of the states, run crosswise in a diagonal pattern. The original lands were a gift from the states of Virginia and Maryland. In 1846, however, Virginia took back her portion of land, making the present-day total area of the District of Columbia 69 square miles.

Letters and notes accompanying l'Enfant's plans show a definite purpose in every aspect of his design. He wrote:

... a street laid out on a dimension proportioned to the greatness which the Capital of a powerful Empire ought to manifest."[1]

The magnificence of Versailles prompted l'Enfant's grandiose ideas for the young nation's capital.[2] His broadest avenue of 400 feet has now become the grassy expanse separating the northern and southern rows of buildings which comprise the Smithsonian Institution.[3] A unique privilege of excelling the height of the Capitol's dome was granted the Washington Monument. At 555-feet, 5.125-inches, the obelisk serves to salute the father and founder of this nation. An aluminum cap atop the monument shouts out its own song of praise and worship to our God and Father. An inscription upon it bears the Latin words *Laus Deo,* that is to say: "Praise be to God!"

In 1800, the government moved from Philadelphia to Washington with its 126 workers, 32 Senators and 106 Representatives. Before the move, eight other capitals had been evidenced as follows: Albany, New York, Philadelphia, Baltimore, York, Princeton, Annapolis and Trenton.

Chapter 1

Unless the Lord builds the house its builders labor in vain. Unless the Lord watches over the city, the watchmen stand guard in vain. — Psalm 127:1,2

First Tour:
Laying the Foundation

National Archives • Jefferson Memorial • Washington Monument

As the Declaration of Independence, the Constitution and the Bill of Rights form the foundational documents of our nation, it is fitting that we begin our first tour at the National Archives Building, situated at Constitution Avenue between 7th and 9th Streets, N.W., where these original writings are housed.

The two historical figures most closely associated with these documents are Thomas Jefferson, author of the Declaration of Independence; and George Washington, first President of the United States.

Jefferson is immortalized at the Jefferson Memorial, located on the South Shore of the Tidal Basin, West Potomac Park.

The Washington Monument is a fitting tribute to our first President. This impressive obelisk is at the center of the Mall, Constitution Avenue at 15th Street, N.W.

The National Archives

As we approach this classic building, the following poignant words of wisdom are inscribed on statues flanking each side of the Constitution Avenue entranceway of our National Archives:

17

At the National Archives — the statue "Heritage."

"Eternal Vigilance is the Price of Liberty" and "The Heritage of the Past is the Seed that brings forth the Harvest of the Future"

On the upper, central attic wall, facing Constitution Avenue, we glean the following message:

The ties that bind the lives of our people in one dissoluble union are perpetuated in the Archives of our government and to their custody this building is dedicated.

Upon the left-hand side exterior attic walls, the purpose for which our National Archives came into being is clearly outlined in two-feet tall lettering:

The Glory and Romance of our History are here Preserved in the Chronicles of those who conceived and builded the Structure of our nation.

The right-hand exterior attic walls show forth its function:

This building holds in trust the records of our national life and symbolizes our faith in the permanency of our national institutions.

Construction for the National Archives building, designed by architect John Russell Pope, began in 1932, and was completed in 1937. Handsome Corinthian columns encircle the structure. Two seated statues flanking its main entranceway represent "Heritage" and "Guardianship." Both sculptures were the work of James Earle Fraser. The neoclassical female figure entitled "Heritage" symbolizes the role of the Government in defending the sanctity of the home and family. The woman holds a child and a sheaf of wheat in her right hand, while the urn under her left hand symbolizes the Home. Guardianship is represented by a male personage holding in one hand the helmet of protection and in the other, a sheathed sword, together with "fasces," the Roman symbol of Unified Government.

Two 38-foot, 7-inch tall bronze doors, each weighing 6.5 tons, slide into the walls, only to be seen before or at the close of a working day.

You will walk over a large, circular, bronze design in the floor as you enter the building. The four allegorical, winged figures represent Legislation, Justice, History, and War and Defense — indicative of the documents housed within this structure. Interestingly enough, God's magnificent Ten Commandments stand out in prominence with the "Senate" and "Justice" to the right, symbolizing our legal system and showing forth from whence our power is derived.

Upon entering the Rotunda, one is greeted by two large murals on either side, entitled: "The Declaration of Independence," and "The Constitution" which were painted by New York's Barry Faulkner in the 1930's.

The Rotunda, or Great Hall, houses three items of great value preserved in helium-filled bronze and glass display cases. These are the original, handwritten parchments upon which our democracy is based: The Declaration of Independence, The Constitution, and The Bill of Rights.

The Declaration of Independence, forerunner of our Constitution, is founded upon the Word of God. Composed by Thomas Jefferson, it begins with an acknowledgment that man's freedom and equality was bestowed upon him by Almighty God.

> We hold these truths to be self evident, that all men are created equal, that they are endowed by their Creator with certain unalienable rights, that among these are Life, Liberty, and the Pursuit of Happiness — That to secure these rights governments are instituted among men, deriving their just powers from the consent of the governed, that whenever any form of Government becomes destructive of these ends, it is the right of the people to alter or to abolish it, and to institute new government, laying its Foundation on such principles, and organizing its powers in such form as to them shall seem most likely to effect their safety and happiness ...

A compilation of 27 grievances against the current power are then cited, after which a final conclusion is drawn:

> We therefore, the representatives of the United States of America, in General Congress, assembled, appealing to the Supreme Judge of the World for the rectitude of our intentions, do, in the name and by authority of the good people of these colonies, solemnly publish and declare, that these united colonies are, and of right ought to be, free and independent states ... And for the support of this Declaration, with a firm reliance on the Protection of Divine Providence, we mutually pledge to each other our lives, our fortunes and our sacred honor.
>
> Signed by order and in behalf of the Congress,   **John Hancock, President**

We now move on to the Jefferson Memorial, the next stop on this tour. A replica of the Pantheon in Rome, it justly pays tribute to the author of the Declaration of Independence, Thomas Jefferson.

The Jefferson Memorial

> I have sworn upon the altar of God eternal hostility against every form of tyranny over the mind of man.   **Thomas Jefferson, President, United States of America**

As first vice president and third president of the United States, Thomas Jefferson's genius extended itself into the realm of law, letters, invention and architecture. His penchant in architectural design is exemplified in the circular, dome-shaped colonaded lines of the Jefferson Memorial. Its classic style reflects Jefferson's admiration for the Pantheon in Rome, as also evidenced in similar designs of the Virginia State Capitol, the Rotunda of the University of Virginia, and Monticello, his gracious home outside Charlottesville. John Russell Pope served as architect in its construction. In 1943, the 200th anniversary of Jefferson's birth was celebrated with the inauguration and grand opening of this building to the public.

A sculptured pediment above the entranceway steps to the

The Jefferson Memorial

memorial is the work of sculptor Adolf A. Weinman. Featured in the tableau is Jefferson reading his draft of the Declaration of Independence to the Committee appointed by the Continental Congress to write the document: Benjamin Franklin, John Adams, Roger Sherman and Robert R. Livingston. Centered within the interior, domed structure, is a 19-foot tall bronze statue of Jefferson standing upon a black granite pedestal. He directly faces the south façade of the White House, so it has been said that Jefferson is keenly aware of current proceedings in the President's House. He sports a fur-collared great coat, gift of his friend, General Thaddeus Kosciuszko.

The famous Declaration of Independence is held in his left hand. As you encircle the statue, take note of the two early symbols of colonial prosperity: corn and tobacco, which reflect Jefferson's love of agriculture. The "capitals" above them indicate his interest in architecture. The sculptor is Rudulph Evans of New York. Viewed from the outside, the Vermont White marble exterior of the memorial reaches a height of 96 feet, the building being 152 feet in diameter. Its beauty is enhanced by 650 Japanese flowering cherry trees which adorn the Tidal Basin. They represent *Yoshino* (white) and *Akebonos* (pink) cherry trees, a gift from the city of Tokyo to the city of Washington. There were originally 3,000 of these given. The first two trees were planted on March 27, 1912, by Mrs. William Howard Taft and Viscountess Chinda, wife of the Japanese Ambassador to the United States.

Inscribed in a circular pattern within the inner dome, in bold letters, are the words:

> "I have sworn upon the altar of God eternal hostility against every form of tyranny over the mind of man."

Four interior wall panels immortalize Jefferson's ideals and concepts. These quoted excerpts originate from the Virginia Statute for Religious Freedom; the Declaration of Independence; Jefferson's views on slavery; and his advocacy that institutions and organizations should advance with the progress of a civilization. An excerpt taken from the Virginia Statute for Religious Freedom reads:

> "Almighty God hath created the mind free. All attempts to influence it by temporal punishments or burthens ... are a departure from the plan of the Holy Author of our Religion ... "

Another panel depicts Jefferson's elaboration upon slavery, viewed from God's eyes:

"God, who gave us life gave us liberty. Can the liberties of a nation be secure when we have removed a conviction that these liberties are the gift of God? Indeed I tremble for my country when I reflect that God is just. That His justice cannot sleep forever. Commerce between master and slave is despotism. Nothing is more certainly written in the book of fate than these people are to be free. Establish the law for educating the common people this it is the business of the state to effect and on a general plan."

A third panelled inscription conveys a familiar message, taken from the Declaration of Independence:

"We hold these truths to be self evident. That all men are created equal. That they are endowed by their Creator with certain inalienable rights. Among these are life, liberty, and the pursuit of happiness, that to secure these rights governments are instituted among men. We ... solemnly publish and declare that these colonies are and of right ought to be free and independent states ... And for the support of this declaration, with a firm reliance on the protection of Divine Providence, we mutually pledge our lives, our fortunes and our sacred honour."

A fourth panel indicates the author's belief that laws and institutions within a society should advance hand in hand with the progress of the times.

The reader is struck by Jefferson's repeated mention and emphasis upon Almighty God and His attributes as man's Creator; The Holy Author of our Religion; the God of our life and liberty, our freedom coming as a gift from God; and the awesome justice of God. His was a profound respect and reverential awe of the Creator of heaven and earth, whom he acknowledged to be the founder and keeper of America's amazing democratic way of life, her liberty and her freedom to pursue happiness ... that is within the sphere of God's protective covering.

Our last stop on this tour is the Washington Monument, which memorializes the instrument God chose to form and fashion a unique new system of government.

The Washington Monument

... with its stately simplicity and the high qualities of manhood it honors, it is fitting that the aluminum tip that caps it should bear the phrase "Laus Deo."

William Howard Taft , President, United States of America[1]

On the aluminum cap atop the Washington Monument are inscribed the words *Laus Deo,* that is to say, "Praise be to God!"[2]

At a height of 555-feet, 5.125-inches, the monument to the father of our nation overlooks the 69 square miles which comprise the District of Columbia, capital of the United States of America. Construction began in 1848 with President James Knox Polk pre-

The Washington Monument

siding at the laying of the cornerstone. An interval of almost 25 years ensued before the completion of the obelisk, which accounts for a slight change of color at a height of 150 feet. Stone continued to be quarried from the original site outside Baltimore, Maryland, but after a lapse of more than 20 years the level of stone had dropped, thus accounting for its change in hue. The monument is made up entirely of marble and granite with no steel shafts as interior support whatever. Its unique simplicity is enhanced by 50 United States flags proudly encircling the base, each one representing one of the 50 states in the Union.

October 9, 1888, marked the official inauguration and opening of this monument to the public. An original steam elevator took 15 minutes to reach the top, whereas the present electric one reaches the summit in a mere 70 seconds. A panoramic view of the city can be enjoyed at this elevation in height, with maps and sketches outlining each segment of the capital. Pierre Charles l'Enfant's original plan in operation is thus clearly seen. From this vantage point, a perfect cross can be traced, with the White House to the north; the Jefferson Memorial to the south; the Capitol to the east and the Lincoln Memorial to the west.

There are 898 steps and 50 landings. Of the 190 memorial stones inserted within its inner staircase walls, several glorify God in word and deed.

On the Twelfth Landing we read:

"Anno 1850. By the City of Baltimore. May Heaven to this Union continue its beneficence; may brotherly affection with Union be perpetual; may the free Constitution which is the work of our ancestors be sacredly maintained and its administration be stamped with wisdom and virtue." [3]

On the 20th Landing, a memorial stone offered by a company of Christians from China compares Washington with great men of Chinese history:

"It is evident that Washington was a remarkable man. In devising plans he was more decided than Chin-Sing or Wu-Kang; in winning a country, he was braver than Tsau-Tsau or Lin Pi." (Engraved at Ningpo, in the province of Che Heang, China, this third year of the reign of the Emperor He-en Fung, 6th month and seventh day. July 12, 1853.) [4]

On the 21st Landing, a memorial stone conveys this simple message:

"Georgia Convention 1850. Wisdom, Justice, Moderation." [5]

On the 24th Landing, stones offered by Sunday School children from churches in New York and Philadelphia quote Proverbs 10:7,

"The memory of the Just is Blessed."

A preached gospel; a free press, and a searching of the Scriptures is advocated. Two beautiful Scriptures are then cited:

"Suffer the little children to come unto Me, and forbid them not, for of such is the kingdom of God." (Luke 18:16); and "Train up a child in the way he should go, and when he is old he will not depart from it." (Proverbs 22:6)[6]

When the cornerstone of the Washington Monument was laid, on Independence Day, 1948, deposited within its recess were many items and documents of value. Among these are: a copy of the Holy Bible, presented by the Bible Society, instituted in 1816; an American silk flag; the coat of arms of the Washington family; copies of the Constitution and Declaration of Independence;United States Presidents' messages to date of cornerstone laying; likenesses of all Presidents and their inaugural addresses to same date; a portrait of Washington taken from Gilbert Stuart's famous painting; and Daguerreotype likenesses of Gen. and Mrs. Washington.[7]

In an era when men are easily commended for good citizenship and right living, a backward glance at the origins and foundational strength of our country is exemplified in Washington's general orders, which reflect the caliber and moral rectitude which led to the formation of a unique democracy; one which had the boldness to establish itself as the "one nation, under God."

All Officers, non-commissioned Officers and Soldiers are positively forbid playing at Cards, and other games of Chance. At this time of public distress, men may find enough to do in the service of their God, and their Country, without abandoning themselves to vice and immorality ... and it may not be amiss for the troops to know, that if any infamous Rascal in time of action, shall attempt to skulk, hide himself or retreat from the enemy without orders of his commanding Officer; he will instantly be shot down as an example of Cowardice: On the other hand, the General solemnly promises, that he will reward those who shall distinguish themselves, by brave and noble actions; and he desires every Officer to be attentive to this particular, that such men may be afterwards suitably noticed.

George Washington, President, United States of America[8]

Such was the discipline and moral direction given by the founder and first President of our democratic state. An oft-quoted question which arises at this juncture of America's history, is the following: Does Washington's concept, belief and intent for America reflect the United States of today? Was not his America the one country in the world established under the guidance, direction and banner of Almighty God, to whom was given all praise, honor and worship by the great men who formed and fashioned her pivotal foundations? The answer to this question is perhaps to be found in the inaugural Scripture chosen by the 40th President of the United States on January 20, 1981; and January 20, 1985: [9]

" ... if My people who are called by My name, humble themselves and pray, and seek My face and turn from their wicked ways, then I will hear from heaven, and will forgive their sin, and will heal their land." II Chronicles 7:14

It is fitting here that we pause a moment to reiterate George Washington's prayer for America:

"Almighty God; We make our earnest prayer that Thou wilt keep the United States in Thy holy protection; that Thou wilt incline the hearts of the citizens to cultivate a spirit of subordination and obedience to government; and entertain a brotherly affection and love for one another and for their fellow citizens of the United States at large.

"And finally that Thou wilt most graciously be pleased to dispose us all to do justice, to love mercy, and to demean ourselves with that charity, humility, and pacific temper of mind which were the characteristics of the Divine Author of our blessed religion, and without a humble imitation of whose example in these things we can never hope to be a happy nation. Grant our supplication, we beseech Thee, through Jesus Christ our Lord. Amen."

The White House

Chapter 2

I Pray Heaven to Bestow the best of Blessings on this House and all that shall hereafter inhabit it. May none but Honest and Wise Men ever rule under this Roof.

John Adams, President, United States of America [1]

Second Tour:
Government of the Nation

White House • Supreme Court • Capitol •
• Library of Congress • Congressional Cemetery

Of all the public buildings in the new capital city, the cornerstone for the President's House was the first to be laid. This took place in 1792. L'Enfant's original three-point plan incorporated the President's House, executive branch of our government, the Capitol, its legislative branch, and a monument in honor of George Washington, first President of the United States.

Of the designs submitted for this mansion which was to accomodate the first officer of the United States and his family, one was by a mysterious Mr. A.Z., later known to be Thomas Jefferson; another by a certain James Diamond of Somerset County, Maryland, and one by James Hoban, Irishman born in County Kilkenny, Ireland. [2] Hoban received an award for his design which won the competition sponsored by the commissioners of the District of Columbia. [3]

The north facade of this spacious mansion is said to resemble Leinster House in Dublin, Ireland. It is constructed of sandstone from Aquia Creek in Virginia and now comprises 132 rooms and 20 baths. The south facade of the mansion resembles the Chateau de Rastignac in the Perigord, France. [4] The design is Palladian in style and comes from the famous Italian architect, Andrea Palladio.[5]

29

Courtesy of the White House Collection

John Adams' Prayer — On the State Dining Room mantel

The magnificent south balcony is where Heads of State are received by the President of the United States, and where they deliver their public addresses to a large crowd assembled on the South Lawn during official state visits. An inspection of the military guard ensues, while the Marine Corps band adds color, music and pageantry to this splendid tradition.

The President's helicopter alights on the South Lawn.

The first President to occupy this home was John Adams, second President of the United States. When Adams first arrived at his new residence on November 1, 1800, he penned these words to his wife, Abigail:

"I pray heaven to bestow the best of blessings on this House, and all that shall hereafter inhabit it. May none but honest and wise men ever rule under this roof."

His magnificent prayer was carved into the State Dining Room mantel by President Franklin Delano Roosevelt, many years later.

Shortly after she arrived at the President's House to join her husband, Abigail Adams poured out her heart to her daughter, describing her new surroundings:

> Not one room or chamber is finished of the whole. It is habitable by fires in every part, thirteen of which we are obliged to keep daily or sleep in wet and damp places. To assist us in this great castle, and render less attendance necessary, bells are wholly wanting ... and promises are all you can obtain. This is so great an inconvenience that I know not what to do ... We have not the least fence, yard or other convenience, without, and the great unfinished audience room (East Room) I make a drying room of, to hang up the clothes in.[6]

Abigail made the best of her new role as First Lady, however, adding:

> You must keep all this to yourself, and when asked how I like it, say that I write you the situation is beautiful, which is true ... It is a beautiful spot, capable of every improvement, and the more I view it, the more I am delighted with it.[7]

Today, the East Room is the largest room in the White House and is used for State balls, receptions, press conferences, and many other special events. Several weddings have occurred in this beautiful room, to include those of Nellie Grant, Alice Roosevelt and Lynda Bird Johnson. This was also the historic scene of funeral services for Presidents William Henry Harrison, Zachary Taylor, Abraham Lincoln, Warren G. Harding, and Franklin Delano Roosevelt. Displayed here is the most distinguished portrait in the house, that of George Washington, painted by Gilbert Stuart. Dolley Madison had the foresight and presence of mind to have the canvas taken out of its frame and moved to safety during the 1812-1814 war, when the British set fire to all the public buildings in Washington.[8] Afterwards, in order to camouflage the charred walls, the house was repainted white. It was only in 1905, however, that the mansion gained its new, official name: "The White House." [9]

Facing the north entrance, a white corridor serves to connect the main part of the mansion with the President's Oval Office, from where he makes his appearances on television. To the right of the Oval Office is the Old Executive Office Building, which serves the administrative needs of the White House, together with the New Executive Office Building a block away.

Each Christmas marks the anniversary of the "Pageant of Peace," begun by President Calvin Coolidge. The ceremonies commence with a lighting of the National Christmas tree, a lovely Colorado blue spruce, which directly faces the White House South Lawn from its location on the north side of the Ellipse.[10] Each year, fifty smaller trees form a wide semi-circle on either side, one for each state in the Union. Since 1923, almost every President of the United States has been involved in these ceremonies.[11] Winston Churchill participated in the joyful event of 1941, while visiting Washington after Pearl Harbor. President Harry Truman lit the tree by remote control switch from his native Missouri.[12]

Every four years a President is inaugurated into office. He takes and oath of allegiance to uphold the Constitution of the United States with his left hand upon the Bible.

Theodore Roosevelt's inaugural Bible contains an inscription to his son:

"To Theodore Roosevelt, Jr., from his father March 4th, 1905."

Above it are the words:

"I certify that this Bible was used by me in administering the Oath of Office, to Theodore Roosevelt as President of the United States on the 4th day of March, A.D. 1905."[13]　　　**(signed) Melville W. Fuller, Chief Justice of the United States**

William Howard Taft's Bible contains this inscription:

I, William Howard Taft, do solemnly swear that I will faithfully execute the office of President of the United States, and will to the best of my ability, preserve, protect and defend the Constitution of the United States　　**(signed) William Howard Taft**

I certify that this Bible was used by me in administering the oath of office to William Howard Taft as President of the United States, on the 4th day of March, Nineteen hundred and nine [14]　**(signed) Melville W. Fuller, Chief Justice of the United States**

The inscription in Eisenhower's Bible reads:

Presented to Dwight David Eisenhower upon his graduation from U.S.M.A., June, 1915.

Coolidge penned these lines in his first Bible:

"This Bible lay on the table under my hand when I took the oath of office as President, at Plymouth, August 3, 1923.　　　　**(signed) Calvin Coolidge"**[15]

Supreme Court of the United States

Across from the Capitol grounds stands the Supreme Court of the United States. From the year 1801 the Supreme Court was housed in various locations within the Capitol building until the grand opening of its present building in 1935. The exterior façade of the new building consists of white marble from Vermont. It was designed by Cass Gilbert to resemble a neoclassical Roman Temple. A seated figure entitled: "The Authority of Law," to the right, and its female counterpart, "The Contemplation of Justice," to the left, flank the main steps to its entrance. James Earle Fraser was the sculptor of these two

The Ten Commandments

The Struggle between Good & Evil with Good Prevailing

Courtesy of the Supreme Court of the United States

Justice, the Guardian of Liberty— Marble bas-relief work inside and outside the Supreme Court portray such themes as "The Ten Commandments" above the Chief Justice's head, and "Justice, the Guardian of Liberty" with Moses holding the two tablets of the Law in the center.

statues. The female statue is carved from a single piece of marble weighing fifty tons.

A letter addressed to the Architect of the Capitol dated February 12, 1942, gives Fraser's description of his creation as follows:

> The figure is enveloped in thought. The small statue she holds at her side is the symbol of justice which indicates on what she is thinking ... it is a realistic conception of what I consider a heroic type of person with a head and body expressive of the beauty and intelligence of justice.[16]

One gains access to the inner courtroom through a majestic oak doorway. Each door has beautifully engraved upon its lower half the Ten Commanments of Almighty God. (Exodus 20.)

The Inner Courtroom of the Supreme Court shows four marble bas-relief panels beneath the ceiling on each of the four walls. Each has a particular story to tell. The panel directly above the bench where Chief Justice William Rhenquist and the eight Associate Justices are seated, depicts "The Power of Government," and "The Majesty of the Law." Between these two allegorical figures, the Ten Commandments stand out in a position of prominence. The seated figure representing "The Power of Government" has his elbow squarely resting upon God's Ten Commandments. Directly facing the scene, on the opposite wall, a struggle between good and evil is depicted, with Security, Harmony, Peace, Charity and Defense of Virtue triumphing over Corruption, Slander, Deceit, and Despotic Power. This marble bas-relief panel is entitled: "The Struggle Between Good and Evil, With Good Prevailing."

"Justice, the Guardian of Liberty," is the title to the East pediment of the building, A stark reminder of the origin and basis for our American legal system is depicted in the central figure of Moses holding the two tablets of the Old Testament Law, one in either hand.

The Book of the Law, or the Pentateuch, as it is also called, comprises the first five books of the Old Testament: Genesis, Exodus, Leviticus, Numbers and Deuteronomy. God promised unfailing loyalty and love to Joshua, just as He had shown to His servant Moses.

A recurring theme of the Old Testament is success and prosperity based upon meditation and constant striving to abide by the perfect Law of God. The New Testament, being a fulfillment of the Old, only reinforces God's words. The Messiah Himself states that He did not come to abolish the Law but to fulfill it.

The Capitol

"… not the smallest jot or tittle shall pass away from the Law, until all is accomplished." (Matthew 5:17,18) The jot and tittle are the tiniest markings in the Hebrew alphabet.

The Capitol

A pause on the east steps of the Capitol Building gives insight into the purpose for which our government was created. The triangular pediment directly above this traditional site for the inauguration of United States Presidents, depicts a scene entitled: "The Genius of America." Armed America stands in the center with a spear behind her, and a shield bearing "U.S.A." upon it. She gazes at Hope, to the right, who beckons to her to proceed. However, America points towards Justice, to the left, who holds a pair of scales in her left hand and a scroll in her right, reading: "Constitution, 17 September 1787." The message conveyed here is that without justice, there is no hope for America, our justice being based upon the Constitution, which is based upon the Declaration of Independence, which in turn is based upon the justice of God's words.

The Rotunda of the Capitol, with its impressive dome, stands before us, with the House of Representatives to the left and the Senate to the right. Nineteen and a half feet tall, bronze, Armed Freedom stands atop the dome. The work of talented sculptor Thomas Crawford, she holds a sheathed sword in her right hand and a wreath and a shield in her left. Her flowing robes are held together with a buckle bearing the letters: "U.S." Upon her head is a helmet encircled with thirteen stars and an eagle's head and feathers, placed there to camouflage a liberated slave's cap, original concept of the sculptor.

We enter the majestic, domelike interior of the Rotunda through the Christopher Columbus doorway, work of Randolph Rogers. Scenes and main landmarks in the life of this discoverer and explorer of the new world, whose main goal was "to propagate the gospel to unknown coastlands," are depicted upon nine panels. The Rotunda is where Presidents who die in office lie in state before the funeral procession proceeds along Pennsylvania Avenue to the White House, and then to the church of their affiliation. This circular chamber houses eight valuable oil paintings. The four paintings nearest the main entranceway indicate the godly foundations upon which our nation was established. "Landing of Columbus at the island of Guanahani, West Indies, October 12, 1492" portrays a flag with a Latin

The Genius of America — marble sculpture above the East Steps of the Capitol

cross upon it while a friar holds up the Cross of our Lord and Savior Jesus Christ. "Embarkation of the Pilgrims at Delft Haven, Holland, July 22, 1620," by Robert W. Weir is a touching scene of prayer and worship to Almighty God, with bended knee and bowed head. The focal point of this scene aboard ship is an open Bible, the one true guide and source of comfort for the earliest settlers in the land. "God With Us," reads an inscription on the uppermost left-hand sail. (Matthew 1:23) "Baptism of Pocahontas at Jamestown, Virginia, 1613," by John G. Chapman, shows this Indian princess, now immortalized in early Jamestown history, kneeling demurely before a priest, as she awaits baptism into the Christian faith; and "The Discovery of the Mississippi by DeSoto in 1541," portrays a giant crucifix being erected in the presence of native American Indians.

Constantino Brumidi, a political refugee from Rome, envisaged and designed the three-hundred-foot frieze encircling the inner dome of the Rotunda.[17] It stands fifty-eight feet above the stone floor. This unusual masterpiece comprises four hundred years of American history. Beginning with America in History, and the arrival of Christopher Columbus in 1492, each of the sixteen panels depicts an important milestone in the making of the nation's history. Lying upon his back on an elevated scaffolding, Brumidi leaned backwards to gain a clearer perspective of his finished work. A fall from the scaffolding left him holding onto the rung of a ladder, until he could be rescued.[18] It was thus a few months later, in the year 1880, that Brumidi, one of the Capitol's most talented artists relinquished his life. Heart failure, resulting from the fall, caused his death. Brumidi had spent 25 years painting scenes of American history, flora and fauna. His purpose was "to make beautiful the Capitol of the one country on earth in which there is liberty."[19] This he did with deep gratitude to a nation he loved; a nation which had opened its arms wide to him in his hour of need.

His successor, Filippo Costaggini, completed the remaining eight scenes, crowding them to insert his own three historic creations.[20] The Joint Committee on the Library declined his proposition to paint them, however, leaving a blank space in the frieze until the year 1953.[21] At that time, Allyn Cox, official artist to the Capitol, completed the work with later scenes of American history.[22] They comprise the Civil War, the Spanish-American War and the first successful flight undertaken by the Wright brothers in 1903. The majestic grace of this creation, and its equally life-imparting "Apotheosis of George Washing-

Courtesy of the Architect of the Capitol

Columbus, DeSoto — Paintings of famed explorers

Pocahontas, Pilgrims — in Rotunda paintings

ton" in the dome of the Rotunda, are an inspiration to the millions who visit the Capitol each year.

Statuary Hall displays 44 statues of great men and women who helped fashion the life of the nation. Junipero Serra, a Fransiscan friar who brought the good news of eternal life through faith in Jesus Christ to California, stands out in originality. He holds a cross in his right hand and a model mission in his left. Why the mission? San Francisco, San Carlos, San Antonio de Padua, San Diego and others, were originally missionary settlements, established with the purpose of bringing salvation to the lost. What a testimony to the creation of these West Coast cities! Not far from him stands Jason Lee, first missionary to the State of Oregon. He was a prominent minister and statesman who knew the Word of God well and applied it to his life. On the opposite side of the room stands Illinois' Frances E. Willard, founder of the World's Christian Temperance Union in 1883, and associated with Dwight Moody's Evangelistic Movement. Marcus Whitman was a great medical missionary to Washington Territory. Dressed in a pioneer outfit, his Bible under one arm, and his medical equipment in the other hand, this great man of God stood firmly upon the conviction of God's Word. He and his wife Narcissa brought many souls to the Lord, being finally massacred by the Indians in 1847.

While walking along the Senate Connecting Corridor toward the Old Supreme Court Chamber, pause to admire Georgia's Tribute, the statue of Dr. Crawford Williamson Long. He invented the use of suphuric ether as an anesthesia in surgery. Upon the base of the statue are inscribed his own words: "My profession is to me a ministry from God."

After enjoying the elegant and quiet beauty of the Old Supreme Court Chamber (used from 1810 to 1860), take note of a handsome bronze plaque on the adjoining East Wall of the Small Rotunda. Erected on the centennial anniversary of a famous event, it honors Samuel Morse, inventor of the telegraph. He wired the first telegraph message "What Hath God Wrought!" from the Capitol to Baltimore on May 24, 1844.

The House of Representatives

Above the Speaker's Chair in the House of Representatives, an inscription states in whom we place our trust. "In God We Trust," it confidently asserts. On either side of the Speaker's Chair, two life-size portraits catch the viewer's eye. They repre-

Courtesy of the Architect of the Capitol

The Rev. Jason Lee — Oregon hero in Statuary Hall

Courtesy of the Architect of the Capitol

Frances Willard — fought alcohol

Courtesy of the Architect of the Capitol

Junipero Serra — California missionary

sent George Washington and the Marquis de Lafayette. Washington's position of prominence is assured because of the fact that he was the instrument whom God chose to found the United States of America. But what about the portrait of Lafayette? How did it find its place on the left hand side of the Speaker's Chair? This hero of the American Revolution gained entrance by virtue of the fact that he was the first foreigner to address a Joint Session of Congress. [23] The event took place at the time of the Marquis' triumphal return to America in 1824, when he addressed an assembled Congress in what is now called Statuary Hall. [24] A glance at the walls of this crucial center for decision making discloses bas-relief profiles of famous lawmakers of the past. Is it by sheer coincidence, or by Divine Intervention, that the only full face, the head of Moses, to whom Almighty God gave the Ten Commandments, stands out directly opposite the Speaker's Chair — a silent reminder to all who enter of the awesome responsibility placed upon the leaders of the "One nation under God."

Voting within the House of Representatives takes place by means of red, green and yellow buttons behind the delegates' chairs. A swift tally of votes appears upon a plexiglass electronic board above the Reporters' Gallery. The blue damask façade, perfect counterfeit of the remaining wall coverings, lights up and reveals an electronic device of modern-day ingenuity. All 435 delegates are represented with "yea," "nay" or "abstain" signs next to their names. One sits enraptured by the quiet beauty and efficiency of this room where so much power is wielded, and where binding national policies are made.

The Senate

The United States Senate is composed of one hundred Senators, two representing each of the fifty states in the Union. Each elected officer serves a six-year term, on a renewable basis. The Vice President of the United States presides over the Senate. The business of the Senate is generally done by a president pro tempore, however.

Encircling the inner walls are marble busts of twenty Vice Presidents of the United States, all of whom served as President of the Senate. [25]

Dr. Richard C. Halverson has filled the office of Senate Chaplain since February 2, 1981. Addressing a fellowship dinner which took place in conjunction with the 1982 National Prayer Breakfast, Senator Mark O. Hatfield introduced this man in

Courtesy of the Architect of the Capitol

Marcus Whitman — medical missionary

WHAT HATH GOD WROUGHT!

1791 1872

SAMUEL F. B. MORSE
THE INVENTOR

ON MAY 24 1844 IN THE OLD SUPREME COURT ROOM - NOW THE LAW LIBRARY IN THE CAPITOL, - SENT THE ABOVE MESSAGE TO BALTIMORE MARYLAND BY THE FIRST ELECTRO-MAGNETIC TELEGRAPH INSTRUMENT

ON MAY 24 1944 THE SEVENTY-EIGHTH CONGRESS OF THE UNITED-STATES - SECOND SESSION - DEDICATED THIS MEMORIAL TO THE HUMILITY AND VISION WHICH ENABLED THIS INVENTOR TO BE THE CONVEYOR OF THIS UNIVERSAL BLESSING TO MANKIND

Courtesy of the Architect of the Capitol

Samuel Morse — Rotunda plaque honors telegraph inventor

terms of the dynamic simplicity of his opening prayers. In the Senator's words:

"Dick Halverson is the first Senate Chaplain with whom I have been acquainted, whose prayers are heard and listened to by those other than Almighty God."[26]

Here are some of Dr. Halverson's straightforward communications with the Lord:

Monday, November 16, 1981 " ... Gracious God, help us to realize that we need to worship Thee, that it is of the essence of true humanness. Help us to see that in denying Thee, we deny ourselves. In the words of the Apostle Paul: 'Though they knew God they did not honor Him as God, or give thanks to Him, and they became futile in their thinking and their senseless minds were darkened. Claiming to be wise, they became fools.'" Romans 1:2,22 [27]

Thursday, September 16, 1982 "... Father in Heaven, our violent, hostile world is starved for love. Children are starved for love which is their only real security, and wives are starved for love because husbands are too busy being successful. Senate staff are starved for love in an atmosphere of competition and struggle for position and power. Senators are starved for love — everybody that gets to them wants something and they are exploited rather than loved. And, loving Father, the tragedy is that in our culture too often love is considered weakness and rejected as a matter of policy. Remind us Lord, that the most powerful force in history is love and that love on a cross conquered our great enemy death. In the name of Him who is incarnate Love. Amen." [28]

Prayer and Bible Study groups are a common feature of Capitol Hill life. It began on a small scale, with a few committed believers, and has evolved into many regular prayer and Bible Study group meetings. Men and women in leadership, who are committed to their faith in Christ Jesus, meet on a continuing basis to immerse themselves in Scripture; for spiritual growth and a renewal of the mind of Christ. [29]

The Prayer Room

A small private room in the Capitol Building serves as a quiet place of prayer and meditation for Senators and Congressmen who wish to turn their thoughts and minds to spiritual things. The room was completed and opened for use in March of 1955. From various members of the Senate and House of Representatives come the following quotations:

... a place at the Capitol where we might meditate and pray, where the mood of prayer could be encouraged[30]

"We legislators might insist that in no other area are men driven so powerfully as in our profession. How well we do our job in creativeness must be left to the judgment of our contemporaries and of history. But as creatures seeking peace of mind, we should

Courtesy of the Architect of the Capitol

In God We Trust — motto above Speaker of the House's Chair

MOSES

Moses — from the House of Representatives chamber

Prayer Window — in private prayer room for legislators

use the facilities of meditation and prayer with assurance that we will not be mis-judged, that we will be permitted this aid to moral exercise, and that our private devotions will be respected ... "[31]

"One of the finest things that this Congress has done, one of the finest things that any Congress has done, or could do ..."[32]

To date, no less than 13 members of Congress, together with the Architect of the Capitol, have celebrated their marriages in this beautiful setting.[33] A focal point in the room is a handsome stained-glass window, known as the Prayer Window. An oval-shaped central design encloses the figure of George Washington, with hands clasped in prayer. Above the kneeling figure, "This Nation under God" stands out in capital letters. Encircling the symbol of communion with God, are the opening words of Psalm 16:

"Preserve me, O God, for in Thee do I put my trust."

An outer, arch-shaped frame contains the names of our 50 states in the Union. Beneath the figure lost in prayer, the seal of the United States stands out, on the one hand depicting prominence and success, and on the other, subjection to its God and King.

The Library of Congress

Atop our National Library of Congress stands the "Torch of Learning," welcoming all who wish to inquire into the vast array of knowledge which this library has to offer.

The library serves primarily as a research arm for Congress. It was established in 1800 with an appropriation of five thousand dollars. Housed in a small chamber within the Capitol Building, its collection at the outset comprised a mere 740 volumes and three maps.[34] A fire in 1814 destroyed the young library's entire collection. With undaunted perseverance, the library purchased 6,700 books from the private collection of Thomas Jefferson. On Christmas Eve, 1851, however, a second fire destroyed the larger part of this valuable new acquisition. Far from being deterred in its original plan and purpose, the Library of Congress commenced anew. Today, it estimates an approximate collection of 84 million items. Rare book collections (such as those belonging to Tsar Nicholas II and Adolf Hitler); music, recordings, prints, photographs and copyright items are part of the collection.[35]

Over 50 painters, sculptors, and artists were employed in the

What doth the Lord require — in Library of Congress

creation of the present building, which earned for itself the reputation of "the most beautiful building in the world," at its inauguration in 1897. Eight pillars adorn the inner sanctum of the Main Reading Room (which is scheduled to be closed to the public for renovations for at least one year, beginning December 9, 1987). Four of these extol God's greatness. Inscribed above the pillar representing Religion we read:

"What doth the Lord require of thee but to do justly, to love mercy and to walk humbly with thy God?" (Micah 6:8).

Science bears these choice words:

"The heavens declare the glory of God and the firmament showeth His handiwork." (Psalm 19:1).

History formulates the following epitaph:

"One God, one law, one element and one far-off Divine event to which the whole creation moves." (Alfred, Lord Tennyson).

Philosophy has coined its own descriptive words in the language of Bacon:

"The inquiry, knowledge and belief of Truth is the sovereign good of human nature."

Two magnificent bronze statues flank Religion on either side. They are "Moses" for the Old Testament, and "Paul, Apostle to the Gentiles" for the New.

The magnificent dome comprises hundreds of lotus flowers, gilded with 23-carat gold. A painting in the dome depicts past world civilizations and their major contribution to present-day world culture. Among these are: America, whose contribution is Science; Italy-Fine Arts; Germany-the Art of Printing; France-Emancipation; and Judea-Religion. Why religion? Because the Messiah, God's greatest gift to the world, came from Judea. An Israeli muse is portrayed next to this inscription with her hands raised in prayer and praise, the Ten Commandments by her side and the Old Testament Law on her lap.

Two of the world's oldest and most valuable Bibles are on display in the vestibule of this magnificent building. The Gutenberg Bible (1455 A.D.) was the first great Book printed with movable metal type. The library's copy is one of the three vellum copies in existence today. It was acquired through an Act of Congress as part of a private collection belonging to Mr. Otto Volbergh, a Jew living in Nazi Germany during the years preceding World War II. In fair exchange for this valuable heritage, his request for a passport to the United States and one and a half million dollars was granted. The giant Bible of Mainz (1453 A.D.) holds its own unique position of preeminence as a hand-copied masterpiece of exceptional craftsmanship and ingenuity. Fifteen months of meticulous calligraphy demonstrates the scribe's painstaking effort in the completion of his God-given task.

The Congressional Cemetery

A sign welcoming all who enter the peaceful sanctuary of historical Congressional Cemetery states that this is the nation's first national cemetery.

The cemetery displays multiple and varied tombstones, stone crosses and stately monuments to our departed ones, both known and unknown in this world. Among these, are Herbert Lincoln, the world's premier Cornetist and Bandmaster (1867-1945) erected by the Pennsylvania Bandmaster's Association and Friends. Cenotaphs were erected for U.S. Senators Henry Clay of Kentucky; John Calhoun of South Carolina and James Bell of New Hampshire; together with Congressmen John G. Montgomery of Pennsylvania, and James Lockhart of Indiana, among others. Prominent architects who took an active part in designing a number of outstanding buildings in the nation's capital, such as William Thornton (U.S. Capitol) and Robert Mills (The Washington Monument), are also buried here. Noted and beloved American composer John Philip Sousa, whose marching tunes have enchanted millions worldwide, has found his resting place at this site. In the southwest section of the cemetery, the gravesite of a ten-year old girl, Marion Kahlert, whose untimely death was the result of Washington's first motor accident, can be seen. J. Edgar Hoover is also interred here.

Maps and information may be acquired at the entrance to these grounds, in the gatekeeper's house. For those who love original historic sites, don't miss the nation's very first national cemetery.

The National Cathedral

Chapter 3

Third Tour:
The Nation's Cathedral

National Cathedral

At a vantage point of 676 feet above sea level, the *Gloria in Excelsis Deo* tower overlooks l'Enfant's executed plan for the nation's capital city. A ten-bell ring and 53-bell carillon comprise the inner workings of the tower, which measures just over 300 feet. Over 100 angel heads with different hairstyles and facial expressions grace the uppermost part of the tower. "Why so much work, time and effort in the creation of these heavenly messengers, when no one can see their beauty from the ground?" one inquirer asked.

"The important thing is that God sees," replied the sculptor, "And they are there *to glorify His name.*"

The beginnings of the National Cathedral can be traced to Major Pierre Charles l'Enfant's concept of a church in the new federal city, erected for national purposes:

"...a temple for national semi-religious celebrations, such as public prayer, thanksgivings, funeral orations, etc., and assigned to the special use of no particular sect or denomination, but equally opened to all."[1]

In the new nation, nothing was attempted in line of fulfilling his vision. It is reported, however, that Joseph Nourse, one of the first civil officers of the government and personal friend of

57

George Washington, used to pray under the spacious trees of Mount Saint Alban.[2] His prayer was that God would build a church on "Alban Hill" in a future timeframe of His choosing. Long after his death, St. John's School for Boys came into being on this site. The school's upper room became a chapel in which Joseph Nourse's granddaughter taught Sunday School for many years.[3] At her death in 1850, 40 gold dollars were found tucked away in a small box. They represented savings from her needlework sales. Inscribed upon the box were the words: "For a free church on Alban Hill."[4] A fund was begun with these proceeds and schoolboys from St. John's dug the foundation of St. Alban's, the first free church in the District of Columbia.[5]

Over and over again, God's hand protected this plot of land from falling to secular usage, by the presence of the little church of St. Alban's, which stood its ground upon Alban Hill — confident sentinel of what was to come.

Founded as a "House of Prayer for all People," the working out of the Cathedral ideal began in 1893 when Congress granted a Charter to the Protestant Episcopal Cathedral Foundation of the District of Columbia for its construction. In the Preamble to its Constitution, a threefold purpose for the creation of a Cathedral church in the diocese of Washington is stated:

> First. It shall be a House of Prayer for all people, forever free and open, welcoming all who enter its doors to hear the glad tidings of the Kingdom of Heaven, and to worship God in Spirit and in Truth. It shall stand in the Capital of our country as a witness for Jesus Christ, the same yesterday, today and forever, and for the faith once for all delivered to the saints; and for the ministration of Christ's Holy Word and sacraments, which according to His own divine ordinance is to continue alway to the end of the world.
>
> Second. It shall be the Bishop's church in which his Cathedra is placed ...[6]
>
> And thirdly, the fourfold work of the Cathedral is outlined in order of importance: Worship, Missions, Education and Charity.[7]

Its official name is that of the Cathedral Church of St. Peter and St. Paul. In 1907 President Theodore Roosevelt laid the foundation stone of the National Cathedral, which comes from a a field near Bethlehem.

The architects chosen to do this formidable task were Dr. George F. Bodley of London and Henry Vaughan of Boston. The designs and working drawings of the Cathedral since 1920 are the principal undertaking of the architect, Philip Hubert Frohman of Boston and Washington. Mr. Frohman penned these lines:

Here in Washington, D.C., we have unrivaled opportunity of building a great 14th century English Gothic Cathedral, of drawing inspiration from the beginnings of Gothic architecture in the Norman, and of grafting onto this strong tree the flower-like beauty of detail of the 14th century. So we are endeavoring to realize an ideal dimly foreshadowed in the 14th century and hope that we may be able to achieve that which may be a stepping-stone to a development of Gothic architecture in the future — which will be greater and more beautiful than any single period of the past.[8]

An aerial view of the Cathedral discloses the shape of a cross, vivid reminder of our Christian heritage. When completed, the National Cathedral will be slightly smaller than the Cathedral of St. John the Divine in New York, but larger than St. Paul's in London or Notre Dame in Paris. It will be the sixth largest Cathedral in the world.[9] The capacity of our National Cathedral comprises standing room for 3,000 persons and space for more than 2,000 people seated. The vaulted ceiling of the Cathedral extends to an average of 95 feet. The entire exterior and interior façade is constructed of Indiana limestone, while the interior flooring is made up of fine marble. From the west façade to the apse, the Cathedral extends one tenth of a mile.

High up on the nave walls of the Cathedral, flags of our 50 states are displayed. At the principal service each Sunday, they are carried in the processional. Each year, beginning with the first Sunday after Independence Day, the flag of Delaware, first state to join the Union, is carried. This is followed by Pennsylvania, and so on, until all 50 states have been recognized. But what of the two remaining weeks in the year, one might ask? Flags of the District of Columbia and the United States of America are honored during the last two weeks of the year.

The Cathedral's great organ comprises over 10,000 individual pipes. Trumpets over the main altar symbolize an important call to assemble and worship the Most High God.

About sixty volunteers arrange the flowers and take care of the altars in the National Cathedral. There are about 900 volunteers in all who minister to the needs of the Cathedral.

Hundreds of bosses grace the high vaulting of the Cathedral's architecture. These can be described as projecting stones, often ornately carved, at the intersection of ribs. Their function is to tie the ribs together into a single neat unit. One of the three largest bosses, four feet in diameter, illustrates a family grouping with open hymnal, worshipping the Lord in song and praise. Father and daughter share an open songbook, while mother, son and youngest daughter lift up their hands in a gesture of wondrous praise. Another smaller boss depicts the lines of the

Psalm: "O let the earth bless the Lord," and "O ye whales and all that move in the waters, bless ye the Lord."[10]

Themes such as the Good Shepherd, Christ reigning in Majesty and the angel of Revelation 6:5 weighing souls in the scales of Judgment, are here portrayed.[11] The central boss of the crossing shows Christ ascending into heaven, the pivotal doctrines of our faith being sculptured in 24 main bosses from the west portal to the sanctuary itself.[12] Dynamic in their expression and impact, are the bosses depicting, in turn, Christ's arrest, the soldiers casting lots for His garments, a group of despairing disciples, a strong centurion guarding the sealed tomb, and finally, the empty tomb.[13]

The Jerusalem Altar

Impressive in its regal simplicity, the Jerusalem Altar was consecrated on Ascension Day 1902. It is constructed of stone coming from the same quarry outside Jerusalem from which Solomon's Temple was built. This symbolizes a close association with the place of Christ's crucifixion and resurrection. Stones from the chapel of Moses on Mount Sinai are set into the floor before the High Altar, in such a manner as to have the priest stand upon them when a reading of the Ten Commandments is given. One hundred and ten statues are represented in the limestone reredos of this altar. They speak of the many unknown Christians to whom Christ referred in the Bible as follows:

"I was hungry and you fed me. I was thirsty and you gave me drink ... inherit the Kingdom prepared for you from the foundation of the world." (Matthew 25)

A central figure of Christ the Majestic reigns in the midst of these saints, both known and unknown, who loved and served the Lord in this life.

The Glastonbury Cathedra, or Bishop's Chair is formed of stones from the Old Abbey Church of St. Peter and St. Paul in Glastonbury, England, from which our National Cathedral derives its name. It is a solid stone chair to the left of the High Altar, just inside the communion railing, and was given by the congregation of Glastonbury to the Cathedral Church of St. Peter and St. Paul in Washington. The earliest roots of Christianity in England have their origin in Glastonbury, where Joseph of Arimathea is purported to have been the first to preach the gospel.

A 60-foot long communion railing divides the great choir from the sanctuary. Needlepoint kneelers depict images of the fruit of the vine and sheaves of wheat, symbols of the Last Supper. The designs of a Victor's crown, which predominates the crown of thorns, symbolize both the suffering and the glorious resurrection of Christ. Black, red and white butterflies portray the new life which one receives in Christ Jesus. A polished wooden railing displays twelve columns. The eleven pillars of the church are carved to mirror the faithful apostles chosen by Christ. Only Judas Iscariot remains unfinished, a solid piece of wood — mute, and without human form or character. The Canterbury Pulpit is shaped out of stones from Canterbury Cathedral and carved with figures in bas-relief, illustrating the translation of the English Bible, from Alfred the Great to the Revised Version of 1885. It was given in memory of Archbishop Stephen Langton, the first to divide the Bible into chapters and verses.

A Prince Visits the National Cathedral

On May 1, 1981, His Royal Highness, Charles, Prince of Wales, was invited to attend the closing service of a week-long meeting between the Archbishop of Canterbury and the Primates of the Anglican Communion. The needlepoint kneeler used by Charles on this occasion was worked by his grandmother, the Queen Mother, for the War Memorial Chapel. The future King of England gave a well-enunciated and clear reading of II Corinthians 4:1-6 and John 14:6-14.[14] Here are some excerpts from the New Testament reading delivered by Prince Charles on this memorable occasion:

And even if our gospel is veiled, it is veiled to those who are perishing, in whose case the god of this world has blinded the minds of the unbelieving, that they might not see the light of the gospel of the glory of Christ who is the image of God. (II Cor. 4:3-4) and

Jesus said to him: "I am the Way, the Truth, and the Life, no one comes to the Father, but through Me." (John 14:6)

The Chapels of the National Cathedral

Nine chapels radiate the beauty of our Christian heritage. Each plays an active role in the services of the Cathedral. On the ground floor, the War Memorial Chapel, the Children's Chapel, St. John's Chapel, St. Mary's Chapel, and the Chapel of the Holy Spirit open their arms wide to all who pass by. The crypt level offers three exquisite chapels depicting the three main events in the life of Christ the Messiah. These are the Bethlehem, St. Joseph of Arimathea and the Resurrection Chapels, which celebrate, in turn, the Lord's birth, death and triumphant resurrection from the dead. Among those buried in the crypt behind the Joseph of Arimathea Chapel is Helen Keller and her teacher and companion Anne Sullivan. A plaque on the wall designates Helen Keller's date of birth and departure from this life in both English and Braille. The Good Shepherd Chapel — rough-hewn, and reminiscent of Christ's gracious simplicity, is the only chapel in the Cathedral open on a continuing basis for those who wish to lift up their requests and praise to God at any time of day or night.

The War Memorial Chapel

This serves to remind us of our men and women who gave their lives in the armed services, together with the close ties we maintain with England. The Central cross and candlesticks on the altar were a gift from King George VI. Needlepoint kneelers were all worked by English women, to include the Queen Mother, Elizabeth of Great Britain.[15] They were a token of appreciation for America's help during the second World War. To the left of the altar an immense tapestry adorns the east wall. It features seals from each state in the Union and the District of Columbia, Each seal is an individual work of art appliquéd separately to the branches of a sturdy tree.[16] One of the Cathedral's treasured acquisitions, this tapestry measures 9 feet wide by 12 feet long. The five branches of the United States Armed Forces, namely the Army, Navy, Air Force, Coast Guards and Marine Corps form a five point, outside border.[17] The entire work is a masterpiece of American ingenuity. A Latin Cross stands out in centrality above the tree. Eighty-nine women produced the wall hanging, which was designed by the Needlework Studio of Bryn Mawr, Pennsylvania.[18] The 56 individual crosses in a row beneath the tree represent American heroes of past wars, who sacrificed their lives for the cause of freedom.[19]

The Children's Chapel

This was the first of its kind in the world and was given by Mr. and Mrs. Roland L. Taylor of Philadelphia. It was built in memory of their little boy who died at age six, yet who has influenced the lives of countless children to date. An inscription in the chapel reads:

To the glory of God and in loving memory of Roland Leslie Taylor 1905- 1911. Of such is the Kingdom of Heaven.

Everything in this chapel is built to accomodate little people. The miniature organ, chairs and kneelers all reflect their namesake. The low vaulting in the ceiling is full of rich detail, while a gilded wooden reredos portrays Biblical scenes from the New Testament, such as the boy Jesus in the Temple surrounded by religious teachers of his day and later, gathering the little children into His arms. The wrought-iron grille and gates at the entrance to the chapel contain hundreds of animal heads. This theme is carried out in the altar rail kneeler, which features Noah's Ark. Many of God's creatures are exquisitely stitched in pairs upon it. Outlined over the entranceway door are the words: "Suffer little children to come unto Me," with a statue of the boy Jesus extending his hands in a gesture of love, nearby. A miniature stained glass window in the south wall depicts the boyhood stories of David, Samuel and Timothy, together with the lad in whose possession were the five loaves and two fishes. This chapel is a favorite spot for baptisms, having its own child-size baptismal font.

St. John's Chapel

This features needlepoint kneelers designed to honor American scientists, artists, writers, pressmen and statesmen of caliber. A lesson in American history is thus gleaned as the visitor proceeds towards the altar of the chapel. Among celebrated names are those of Thomas Edison, Ottmar Mergenthaler (The News — Linotype); Samuel Houston; Louisa May Alcott; Orvillle Wright (first successful flight from Kitty Hawk, North Carolina); Noah Webster; William Jennings Bryan; Walter Reed; Andrew Carnegie; John J. Audubon; Henry Ward Beecher (Abolitionist, orator, preacher); George Eastman (Camera and film); and Stephen Decatur ("Our Country Right or Wrong"). Each cushion portrays an appropriate symbol for the personality it describes.

Between the row of chairs and the altar railing, on the south wall, a statue of Lieutenant Prince stands out as a memorial to the young man who founded the Lafayette Escadrille in World War I and who lost his life shortly thereafter in this courageous endeavor. Scenes of airplanes and bombs being loaded by hand are depicted beneath the young man's feet. The entire chapel was a gift of the Prince family in memory of their son, Norman Prince. The reredos of St. John's altar takes its theme from the crucified Christ, with the apostle John to the right, and His mother Mary to the left. "Miracle" windows illustrate 28 different miraculous acts of our Lord.

St. Mary's Chapel

Former Ambassador to Belgium, Larz Anderson, was the donor of this graceful chapel. The walls display 15th century Flemish tapestries which depict Biblical scenes of David and Goliath. They tell the incredible story in pictorial form, of the giant Goliath's death through the ingenuity and faith of a young shepherd boy, soon to become King of Israel. Stained glass windows in this chapel relate Christ's message in parabolic form: "Go then and do likewise." This chapel is a favorite spot for weddings, its grace and beauty being exemplified in scenes of the annunciation, the visitation of Mary to her cousin Elizabeth and the celebrated wedding in Cana of Galilee, where Jesus' mother spoke to Him of the need for more wine. Mary is also seen with the disciples in the left hand side, lower sculpture, awaiting the coming of the Holy Spirit upon the young church for empowerment in service. (Acts 1)

The Chapel of the Holy Spirit

The Chapel of the Holy Spirit is a tribute to the third person of the Triune Godhead. The reredos of this altar is a creation of the sculptor and painter, N.C. Wyeth, father of the famous artist, Andrew Wyeth. Choirs of angels are depicted singing their praises to God, and playing musical instruments such as violin, harp and lyre. A gentle dove, symbol of God's Holy Spirit, is shown in various forms of flight or descent, the gifts of the Spirit being inscribed in gold lettering between these symbolic figures, as follows: "Wisdom; Understanding; Counsel; Strength; Knowledge; Godliness; and Holy Fear (Isaiah 11:2). The wrought-iron gate to this chapel is exquisitely hand-fashioned, with graceful peacocks lining its crest.

Stained Glass Windows of the Cathedral

Glorious stained-glass windows shine forth their radiance in exquisite hues of bright reds, oranges, deep azure blues, calm and tranquil sea greens and brilliant yellows.

The National Cathedral Association Windows

These are a memorial to all the devoted Christian women who have given selflessly of their time, talents, and earthly possessions for the furtherance and upbuilding of the Cathedral ideal. They illustrate in vivid imagery, the roles of women as lifegiver, healer, purifier and teacher. The teacher portrayed in the upper portion of the right hand lancet is seen softly explaining some truth to a small child, while pointing heavenward.

The White Memorial Window

A window honoring Gen. Thomas Dresser White and the United States Air Force catches the viewer's eye in a blaze of orange color. Two spread-eagled wings, bright orange in hue, symbolize aircraft in flight, while a solitary tree is the central point for this creation. It tells a poignant story — one which was particularly loved by Gen. White. Brother Lawrence fought as a soldier in medieval times. Returning home after the battle he saw the devastation which the war had caused. He noticed, however, a solitary dry tree which had survived and was coming again into bloom. It reminded him of his dry spiritual life, and that even in the aftermath of battle comes rebirth and new life. Appropriately mirrored in the uppermost lancet of this handsome vitrail is the Air Force Academy Chapel in Colorado.

The Abraham Window

The Abraham Window portrays Abraham's agony as he seeks to obey God in offering his son and heir, Isaac, as a sacrifice upon Mount Moriah. Brilliant golden rays of light above the figure of Isaac tell the Old Testament narrative of an angel from heaven declaring:

"Abraham, Abraham! Do not stretch out your hand against the lad, and do nothing to him, for now I know that you fear God, since you have not withheld your son, your only son, from Me." (Genesis 22:12)

The Lincoln Bay Window

The Lincoln Bay Window expresses the strife and chaos caused by the American Civil War. It is an exquisite composition of darker hues of reds and oranges, rising up to lighter shades of pastel greens and blues. This is an indication of the healing of the nation after the cessation of the war. On the adjacent west wall of the Cathedral, Lincoln's statue stands pensive and silent. Behind it, engraved on the stone surface of the wall, is his farewell address delivered at Springfield, Illinois, on February 11, 1861:

> My Friends: No one, not in my situation, can appreciate my feeling of sadness at this parting, To this place and the kindness of these people I owe everything. Here I have lived a quarter of a century and have passed from a young to an old man. Here my children have been born and one is buried. I now leave, not knowing when or whether ever I may return. With a task before me greater than that which rested upon Washington, without the help of that Divine being who ever attended him, I cannot succeed. With that assistance, I cannot fail. Trusting in Him, who can go with me, and remain with you, and be everywhere for good, let us confidently hope that all will yet be well. To His care commending you, as I hope in your prayers you will commend me, I bid you an affectionate farewell. **(signed) A. Lincoln**

The Washington Bay Window

The Washington Bay Window depicts the foundation and growth of a new nation. Varying shades of green and blue portray the wide, open spaces which characterize America, while droplets of red symbolize the bloodshed and fighting which preceded Independence.

The Woodrow Wilson Bay Window

The Woodrow Wilson Bay Window pays tribute to the memory of the 28th President of the United States. It is the first and largest Bay Window. Seals of the United States, New Jersey and the University of Princeton line the outside facade of the sarcophagus. A crusader's cross represents the struggle for peace after World War I. War and Peace Windows reflect both suffering (to the right) and trust (to the left), as seen upon a child's face. The central lancet portrays the birth of Christ, transforming a chaotic human scene into serenity and peace — reconciliation with God the Father for all who place their trust in Christ's atoning sacrifice.

From a central point in the aisle of the Cathedral, one can admire both the "Creation" window which crowns the West entrance, together with the famed Space Window. Prisms of gorgeous colors fully express the artist's subject of "The Creation of Light." Multi-faceted gems of bright light permeate the window, diffusing it with life. The theme of this window is taken from Genesis 1:1-2:

In the beginning God created the heavens and the earth. And the earth was form-
less and void, and darkness was over the surface of the deep; and the Spirit of God
was moving over the surface of the waters.

A slight turn of the head now gives a full view of the Space
Window also called the Scientist's Window. A large reddish orb
representing the moon, features a central moonrock brought
down to earth by the crew of Apollo 11. This circle is connected
by a trajectory with a smaller, lower globe, symbolizing the
earth. A major part of this unique window radiates varying
shades of rich, royal blues of which our night sky is comprised.
Multiple stars, flung at random into space, give a clear illustration of the artist's theme. A caption beneath Rodney Winfield's
work of art reads:

Is not God in the Height of Heaven?
(from Job 22:12)

Special Features of the National Cathedral Gardens and Grounds

Fifty-seven acres of beautifully landscaped grounds surround
this fourteenth century Gothic splendor. Several landmarks
stand out in their uniqueness and originality, attracting many
visitors.

The Glastonbury Thorn

In 1900, the Reverend Henry Satterlee, first Bishop of Washington, received a cutting of the Thorn from Stanley Austin,
owner of the ruins of Glastonbury Abbey. After returning home
it was planted and carefully nurtured in the Cathedral close,
where it flourished and grew into a sturdy tree.

"The Holy Thorn of Glastonbury" as it is also known,
recounts a legend that can be traced to the staff of Joseph of
Arimathea, who was the first to preach the gospel in England.
Upon his arrival at Yniswitrin, later called Glastonbury, the
saint's staff was stuck in the ground as proof of his intent to
remain. It was this celebrated staff which sprouted leaves and
became the Glastonbury Thorn which blossoms each year at
Christmas. A quaint tradition in England honors each visiting
member of English royalty with a blossom from the tree.[20]

During a visit to Washington in November 1919, the Prince of
Wales was asked if he would like to inspect the Thorn. In keeping with ancient custom, the tree produced a few blossoms for

its royal visitor. Much to his delight, the Prince was presented with a silver box containing a single, prized blossom from the Washington Glastonbury Thorn. A more recent royal guest, Queen Elizabeth of England, was also presented with a blossom from this Thorn tree during her Bicentennial visit to our country.

The Pilgrim Steps

These steps and their planting were a gift of Mr. and Mrs. Roland Leslie Taylor of Philadelphia. They were given in appreciation of all those who helped to further the National Cathedral. Constructed of buff freestone, they originate from a quarry belonging to George Washington in his day. A formal dedication of the steps took place on May 16, 1930. Entrance to the Bishop's garden is thus made through a wrought-iron gate, designed by Samuel Yellin and included as part of the gift. Lettering upon the gate reads: "They shall enter into peace that enter in at these gates."

The Peace Cross

The upraising of the Peace Cross in 1898 commemorated the foundation of the Cathedral of St. Peter and St. Paul, the cessation of the Spanish-American War and also the first meeting of the General Convention in the Nation's Capital. It was thus that the first service to be held on the Cathedral close was attended by thousands of people. The 20-feet tall Iona Cross is made of stone and bears upon its pedestal the words:

"Jesus Christ Himself being the Chief Cornerstone."

The Wheel Cross

This "round-headed" cross is a survival of the early days of Christianity in France. A gift from Mr. George Grey Barnard, the cross is to be seen at the far end of the Bishop's boxwood garden. These early crosses often served as boundary markers or crossroads to guard and guide the visitor along a lonely wayside towards a peaceful church.

The Prodigal Son (the statue of)

The Bishop's garden on the Cathedral close is an inspiration to visit, especially in the spring and summer when blossoms and flowers abound. The Prodigal Son is a unique and masterful interpretation of Christ's parable in Luke 15, of a loose-living and reckless son who returns to his father and rightful home. It stands out in the stark simplicity of its dark granite sculptured lines. German-born Heinz Warneke's interpretation of this powerful analogy of a penitent sinner returning to his loving heavenly Father is well worth seeing and moving to contemplate.

2340 S STREET N W

WOODROW WILSON
WASHINGTON D C

30th July 1923

My dear Dr. Freeman,

Your note of July twenty-seventh was very welcome and I thank you for it warmly.

I am glad to second you in any way possible in accomplishing the completion of the cathedral here. Its completion will not only add greatly to the stately beauty of our national capitol but will provide a center from which I believe, under your guidance, the most useful and beneficial work can be done for the uplift of the community and stimulation of the nation. I hope with all my heart that your efforts in this matter will be crowned with the most complete success.

I hope that you are having a bit of vacation and are gaining real refreshment from it.

I am interested to learn the date of your consecration. It is impossible for me to judge at this distance whether I can be present or not, but even if I am not physically present you may be sure I shall be there in spirit and with warmest hopes for the sort of success on your part which will satisfy both your heart and your mind.

Mrs. Wilson joins me in warm regards, and I beg to subscribe myself,

Your Sincere Friend,

Rev. Dr. James E. Freeman,
Sorrento, Maine.

Woodrow Wilson

Letter from President Woodrow Wilson

GENERAL OF THE ARMIES

WASHINGTON

September
Twenty-eighth
1 9 2 3

Rt. Rev. James E. Freeman, D.D.,
Bishop of Washington,
Washington, D.C.

My dear Bishop Freeman:

As you know it has been a matter
of deep personal regret to me that I could
not arrange my plans so as to participate
in the special services at the Cathedral
Amphitheatre on Sunday. It would have
been a matter of personal satisfaction to
me to be present at this gathering of those
who are dedicating their efforts to complete
the construction of the Cathedral.

As an Episcopalian and as a
Trustee of the Church, it is my hope and
prayer that the magnificent structure
planned to rise on this ground may soon be
a reality, a great monument to the glory
of God, and a visible evidence in the capital of the Republic of the faith of the
people in their religious institutions.

Very sincerely yours,

John J. Pershing

Letter from Gen. John Pershing

THE WHITE HOUSE
WASHINGTON

September 17, 1923.

My dear Bishop Freeman:

I wish to express my thanks to you, and to General Pershing as well, for the courtesy of your call and your cordial invitation to participate in the services at the Episcopal Cathedral on Sunday September 30th. I am most regretful that it is impossible for me to accept the invitation, for the occasion presents a particular appeal to me, and I cannot let it pass without expressing to you my congratulations on the progress you are making in building the Washington Cathedral. It has already become both an adornment and an inspiration in the national capital, and I know that your devotion to the cause which it typifies will be a powerful factor of assurance that the work will proceed in both material and spiritual accomplishment.

Your work is to be commended, because it represents the foundation of all progress, all government, and all civilization. That foundation is religion. Our country is not lacking in material resources, and though we need more education, it cannot be said to be lacking in intelligence. But, certainly, it has need of a greater practical application of the truths of religion. It is only in that direction that there is hope of solution of our economic and social problems. Whatever inspires and strengthens the religious belief and religious activity of the people, whatever ministers to their spiritual life, is of supreme importance. Without it, all other efforts will fail. With it, there lies the only hope of success. The strength of our country is the strength of its religious convictions. To you and all those associated with you throughout our land in ministering to religion, I extend my appreciation of your toil and sacrifice, and my faith in your ultimate success.

Most sincerely yours,

Rev. James E. Freeman,
1329 K Street, N.W.,
Washington, D. C.

Letter from President Calvin Coolidge

Chapter 4

Fourth Tour:
America's National Churches

Metropolitan Methodist Memorial Church • Metropolitan AME Church • National Presbyterian Church • Russian Orthodox Church of America • St. Sophia's Church: The National Greek Orthodox Church of America

Metropolitan Methodist Memorial Church

The idea of a National Methodist Church in the Nation's capital was conceived on May 10, 1852, at a session of the General Conference meeting in Boston. Two years later, on October 23, 1854, the cornerstone for the original church was laid. Among the valued articles deposited within, were: A copy of the Holy Bible, Inaugural Addresses of the first five Presidents of the United States; The Congressional Directory and Proceedings from the Continental Congress.[1]

Funds for the first building, completed in 1869, and situated at John Marshall Place and C Street, N.W., came from churches and individuals throughout the United States, making this a truly national place of worship. Prominent leaders in the government of our nation were among the first trustees of the church, namely: Ulysses S. Grant, President of the United States and first Chairman of the Board; Salmon P. Chase, Chief Justice of the Supreme Court; and Matthew G. Emery, Mayor of the City of Washington at the time.[2]

Construction for the present building was begun in 1930 and

completed in 1932, its architect being Harold E. Wagoner. The regal interior of this church, with its 70-foot high, ornate, vaulted ceiling, hanging chandeliers and pure French Gothic architecture, has been described as "The Westminster Abbey of American Methodism." The exquisite design of the church is enhanced by a tall fleish — a delicate spire reaching into the sky, reminiscent of La Sainte Chapelle in Paris.[3]

In keeping with its national character, special pews are set aside for the President, Vice President and Supreme Court Chief Justice, together with each of the 50 states in the Union, the District of Columbia and American Samoa. Silver plaques near the aisle bear these designations. Should you visit this handsome and welcoming church, you may request to be seated in your own state pew. In the old church, General Grant occupied the President's pew for eight years and President McKinley followed suit from 1897 to 1901.[4]

The design of the interior of this church displays a cross, reminding us of the wooden cross upon which Christ died to ransom our souls.

A unique feature greets the visitor as he steps into the foyer of the impressive church building — a beautiful carved walnut screen embossed with antique glass representing each of the twelve apostles, separates the narthex from the nave.

As you proceed up the nave towards the altar, take time to read and contemplate the memorial plaques to prominent American leaders who are here remembered as faithful followers of Christ. Some of these are listed below:

In memory of the virtues and valor of Ulysses S. Grant, General of the Army and President of the United States. Born 27 April 1822. Died 23 July 1885. His friend George C. Childs erects this tablet as a token of affection while the whole country does honor to his career and character.

To the deathless memory of Major General John Alexander Logan. Six years in the House of Representatives. Three times elected to the Senate of the Untied States. Forty years in official life. Great statesman of the mighty west. Commander of the Army of Tennessee and foremost Volunteer General of the Republic he loved so well. Victorious in arms, illustrious in Council. Esteemed worthy of the highest honors of his country. Noblest type of American manhood, generous, frank, brave, incorruptible patriot, honorable citizen, faithful friend, devoted husband, beloved parent, sincere Christian. "I humbly trust in God. If this is the end, I am ready."

"Jesus calls, I am almost home" Matthew G. Emery Born September 28, 1818;Died October 12, 1901.President of the Board of Metropolitan M.E. Church for thirty-two years. Last Mayor of Washington.

Within the main sanctuary, each bay measures 15 feet wide, and is encased within two pillars. There are 11 bays on each side of the nave. As you contemplate their tall elegance, take note of the four emblems, which repeat themselves over and over again beneath each bay. They are: The Star, representing the visit of the wise men from the east to behold the Christ child; The Cross, symbolizing Christ's incomparable sacrifice of Himself on Calvary's cross; the *Fleur-de-Lis,* typifying the Blessed Trinity; and the Anchor, which is Christ, our Hope of Glory.

The carved wooden pulpit and altar rail come in part from the Garden of Gethsemane and the Mount of Olives, the cedar wood coming from Mount Lebanon.

The focal point of this inspiring church is its limestone altar, upon which rests the great symbol of our faith, the cross of our Lord and Savior Jesus Christ. A central Rose Window directly above the altar represents the descent of the Holy Spirit as a dove, with an encircling Scripture:

"He that believeth in the Son of God hath the witness in Himself." (I John 5:10)

Inlaid in the chancel floor are fragments of building tiles from the ruins of Solomon's Temple in Jerusalem. On the upper walls of the chancel, eight stone carvings illustrate characteristics of the four gospel writers — Matthew, Mark, Luke and John; together with John Wesley, founder of Methodism, and Francis Asbury, a pioneer of American Methodism. Apostles Peter and Paul complete this company of true believers.

The keystone in the Baptistry contains a stone from Jerusalem bearing the inscription "Jehovah Jireh," which translated means: "The Lord Provideth" (from Genesis 22:14) A baptismal stained glass window depicts John the Baptist with the wording: "Behold the Lamb of God" (John 1:36).

One of the most outstanding features of the National Church of Methodism is its magnificent Transfiguration Window, which crowns the entranceway, covering most of that wall. Jesus stands in the center, with Moses to his left and Elijah to His right. Four muses — Faith, Hope, Love and Justice — flank the three central figures; while Peter, James and John are portrayed below by their symbols. The entire composition consists of seven vertical lancets with elaborate stone tracery joining the whole in a compact and original work of art.

The national character of the building is further exemplified in its Arizona copper roof with Indiana limestone for trim; its

Ohio stone interior; Vermont slate floors, and flagging from Pennsylvania and New York.[5]

Try to fit this church into your itinerary while in the nation's capital. It will inspire you to great heights of worship as you contemplate the beauty and biblical symbolism of its Christian character.

Metropolitan AME Church

The beautiful Metropolitan African Methodist Episcopal Church, designed in the traditional Victorian Gothic architecture, takes its stance in the heart of the nation's capital as a Category II landmark, adding to our historic/Biblical heritage in America. Surrounded as it is by commercial and more modern enterprises, it remains a gem of lovely old architecture, being replete with Black American history.

On a stone pillar directly outside the main entranceway to the church, one is struck by these welcoming words:

Except the Lord build the House, they labor in vain that build it. (Psalm 127:1)

An inscription goes on to explain the African Methodist Church's beginnings and its development. Organized in 1822, the church was rebuilt in 1838 and completed in 1880. The Rev. William Moore was listed as its first pastor. Listed in the National Register of Historic Places on July 26, 1973, this site, originally acquired by members of the Black community in Washington, possesses great value in commemorating the life of the Negro in the United States of America.

"The National Cathedral of African Methodism" traces its origins to 1787 when a group of disheartened Black believers in Philadelphia, desiring to worship God in spirit and in truth without the stigma of segregation, purchased an old blacksmith's shop and started worship services there. They called this church "Bethel," that is to say, House of God.[6] Their first pulpit was an anvil, and their first preacher, Richard Allen, taught himself to read and write, buying back his own freedom and that of his family. This young man, ordained an elder by Francis Asbury, and consecrated first Bishop of the African Methodist Episcopal Church, was born a slave on the farm of Benjamin Chew, in Philadelphia. He accepted Christ as his savior in 1777, at age 17, acquiring his license to preach in 1782, and buying back his freedom for the price of two thousand dollars.[7]

Frederick Douglass, Chief U.S. Administrator for Deeds and

Metropolitan African Methodist Episcopal Church

Contracts and former freedom fighter, held a pew in the sanctuary. His place of worship is now designated by a bronze plaque bearing his name. In 1885, this hero in the annals of American history, had his funeral preached at Metropolitan African Methodist Episcopal Church. Great leaders of our nation have spoken from its pulpit. Among these are Eleanor Roosevelt, William Howard Taft, and Mary McLeod Bethune. Presidents McKinley and Taft helped to pay the first and second mortgages of this house of prayer. Howard University, a noted institution of higher learning in the District of Columbia, has used the sanctuary for its Graduation Ceremonies.[8] In the years preceding Emancipation, escaped slaves who had sought refuge in the church, bought back their freedom as their Christian brothers and sisters "passed the hat." Vestiges of early horsestables remain in the basement of the building, where slaves used to ride out the back door into freedom.[9]

Unusually original stained glass windows within the main sanctuary of the church were installed as a memorial to those from each of the following state conferences who contributed to the building and completion of the present church: Texas; Oklahoma; Florida; Georgia; N. Carolina; S. Carolina; New England; Indiana; Philadelphia; Baltimore; New York; Ohio; Missouri; California; Louisiana; Virginia; Pittsburgh; Tennessee; Arkansas; Mississippi; Iowa; S. Kansas; N. Ohio; W. Kentucky; N. Alabama; Columbia, S.C.; S. Arkansas; W. Tennessee; N. Georgia; N. Jersey; N. Louisiana; N. Missouri; Indian; N.E. Texas; E. Florida; N. Mississippi; Kansas; West Texas; Illinois; Alabama.

Three arched-shaped stained glass windows in the rear of the church memorialize the inauguration of important functions in the church's life and outreach. They are worded thus:

Missionary Department Organized 1844
Educational Department Oraganized 1876
Sunday School Department Organized August 11, 1882

This historic and highly interesting church was the first Black church founded on American soil. While in the nation's capital, a visit to the "National Cathedral of African Methodism" should inspire and enthuse Christians of all walks with the veracity of Thomas Jefferson's own words:

God who gave us Life, gave us Liberty. Can the Liberties of a nation be secure when we have removed a conviction that these liberties are the Gift of God? Indeed I tremble for my country when I reflect that God is just. That His justice cannot sleep forever. Commerce between master and slave is despotism ... **Thomas Jefferson, President, United States of America** (Inscribed within the Jefferson Memorial)

The National Presbyterian Church

The National Presbyterian Church traces its origins to 1795, when a small group of Scottish masons working on the construction of the new "President's House," moved their weekly worship services from a carpenter's shed to private homes. They named their congregation "St. Andrew's Church." The Reverend John Brackenridge was appointed as first pastor. In 1812, at the site where the present Rayburn House of Representatives Office Building now stands, a simple frame edifice was constructed on the south slope of Capitol Hill. Because of its location, it was called "the little white church under the hill." With a steadily growing membership, the First Presbyterian Church of Washington sprung up in 1827, on $4^{1}/_{2}$ Street, N.W. Its loyal congregation worshipped for the last time in their beloved church on May 11, 1930, the area now being flooded with government property.

The dream of many Presbyterians nationwide was to build a national church at the seat of government. This dream was finally realized when in October, 1947, President Harry S. Truman publicly proclaimed the reality of a National Presbyterian Church in the nation's capital. In keeping with Truman's proclamation, President Dwight D. Eisenhower laid the cornerstone to this handsome, neo-Gothic edifice constructed on October 14, 1967. The first service was held here on September 7, 1969.

The 173-foot tall Tower of Faith, stretches into the sky, greeting all who come nigh. At a height of 573 feet above sea level it houses the "Arlington" Carillon with 61 Flemish bells and 25 bells of English-type tuning. The fountain at the center of the sunken garden is designed to resemble the seal of the United Presbyterian Church in the U.S.A. Three adjacent Alabama stone walls in semicircular formation present the visitor with calligraphied Scriptures. Christ's beautiful words, as recorded in John's gospel, are traced out on the center wall:

If you love me, you will keep my Commandments And I will pray the Father and He will give you another counselor, to be with you forever, even the Spirit of Truth, whom the world cannot receive because it neither sees Him nor knows Him; You know Him for He dwells in you and will be with you. I will not leave you desolate; I will come to

At the National Presbyterian Church — "First, a prayer in Congress," proclaims this beautiful stained-glass window.

you. Yet a little while and the world will see me no more, but you will see me; because I live, you will live also.(John 14:15-19) Revised Standard Version of the New Testament

The left-hand side wall displays excerpts from Psalm 90, which speaks of God's eternity and man's transitoriness.

Lord, thou hast been our dwelling place in all generations. Before the mountains were brought forth, or ever thou hast formed the earth and the world. Even from everlasting to everlasting, thou art God. O satisfy us early with thy mercy that we may rejoice and be glad all our days. Let thy work appear unto thy servants, and thy glory unto their children. And let the beauty of the Lord our God be upon us and establish thou the work of our hands upon us yea, the work of our hands establish thou it. (Psalm 90:1,2,14,16 and 17) King James Version of the Old Testament

The right-hand side wall reiterates the apostle Paul's words to the Philippians, which he wrote from jail, while under arrest:

Let your bearing towards one another arise out of your life in Christ Jesus. For the Divine Nature was his from the first; yet he did not think to snatch at equality with God but made himself nothing, assuming the nature of a slave. Bearing the human likeness, revealed in human shape, he humbled himself, and in obedience accepted even death — death on a cross. Therefore, God raised him to the heights and bestowed on him the name above all names, that at the name of Jesus every knee should bow — in heaven, on earth and in the depths — and every tongue confess, "Jesus Christ is Lord' to the glory of God the Father. (Philippians 2:5-11) New English Version of the New Testament

Upon entering the church through the Reformer's corridor, meaningful prayers of four great saints now with their Lord, come into full view mounted upon pillars. The first of these was communicated by Augustine of Hippo in the fifth Century A.D.

Eternal God who so carest for every one of us as if Thou carest for Him alone and so for all as if all were but one: Blessed is the man who loveth Thee, and his friend in Thee, and His enemy for Thee. For He alone loses no one dear to Him. To whom all are dear in Him who never can be lost. Amen. (A Prayer of Augustine — Fifth Century)

The second was articulated by a great Italian man of God, filled with the Holy Spirit and with love — Francis of Assisi, who lived in the twelfth century A.D.

Lord, make us instruments of Thy peace; where there is hatred let us sow love; where there is injury, pardon; where there is discord, union; where there is doubt, faith; where there is despair, hope; where there is darkness, light; where there is sadness, joy, for thy mercy and for thy truth's sake. Amen. (A prayer of St. Francis of Assisi - 12th Century)

The third comes from the heart and mind of Martin Luther, great 16th century reformer of the church:

Lord, preserve thy people. Maintain righteous government everywhere, so that all things may take place in an orderly way and peace may not be destroyed by revolution or secret enmity. Nor the eternal good order by corrupted and debased living or disturbed by other offenses. Amen.(A Prayer of Martin Luther — 16th Century)

The fourth and last prayer was spoken by another strong man of faith and conviction, who based his life upon the words of God:

Increase our faith, O merciful Father, that we do not swerve at any time from Thy heavenly words, but augment in us hope and love with a careful keeping of all Thy Commandments, that no hardness of heart, no hypocrisy, no concupiscence of the eye, no enticement of the world, do draw us away from Thy Obedience. Amen. (A Prayer of John Knox — 16th Century)

The Chapel of the Presidents

Upon entering this chapel, a simple communication to Almighty God by Dwight D. Eisenhower, stands out in bronze bas-relief upon the outer wall of the foyer. It reads:

Almighty God, give us, we pray, the power to discern clearly right from wrong and to allow all our words and actions to be governed thereby and by the laws of this land.
Dwight D. Eisenhower

The leaders of our nation are prayed for daily at a service in the Chapel of the Presidents. The prayer to Almighty God includes this request:

Look upon thy servant ... The President of the United States, and upon all those in positions of public trust. Empower them to see thy perfect will.

Two main features in this Chapel catch the eye. An Italian white marble baptismal font with the words: "One Lord, One faith, One baptism," repeating themselves in a bronze, circular pattern across the top, come from Paul's letter to the Ephesians, chapter 4, verse 5. The font bears engraved upon its face a sculptured shell and three drops of water, representing the three persons of the Godhead — Father, Son and Holy Spirit. In the stained glass window directly behind it, a ship, emblem of Christ's church on earth, is depicted with the glorious wording: "In the name of God Amen."

Four of the five stained glass windows extending from the floor to the ceiling, to the left of the altar, have these words inscribed on top: "one Nation Under God." Each one bears these words beneath, "We hold these truths to be self evident, that all men are created equal."

Among the great Christian leaders of our country and the world portrayed in these windows are Lord Calvert, William

Penn, Francis Makemie, John Bunyan, Roger Williams, Salzbergers, Muhlenberg and Thomas Jefferson. A far left-hand side lancet depicts a pair of praying hands, golden in hue, with the historical wording surrounding them: "First a Prayer in Congress." The six Presidential stained glass windows show a United States President enacting his Christian faith in the execution of his sacred office as first officer of our country. They are, from left to right: George Washington, Abraham Lincoln, Theodore Roosevelt, Woodrow Wilson, Franklin D. Roosevelt and Dwight D. Eisenhower.

The George Washington Window has inscribed upon its face: "I do solemnly swear that I will faithfully execute the office of President of the United States." It shows the first President being sworn into office with his left hand upon the Bible. The Virginian shows by his act his reverential awe and worship of Almighty God and total allegiance to Him as the Founder and Benefactor of our country. The event took place on April 30, 1789, in New York City. After his swearing in, Washington added the words: "So help me, God," and then kissed the Bible which had been opened at random to Genesis 49-50. Washington thus set a precedence for succeeding Presidents when sworn into office.

He made this declaration himself: "It is impossible to rightly govern the world without God and the Bible." Washington's farewell address strongly supported this principle in the governing of a nation:

> "Of all the dispositions, and habits which lead to political prosperity, Religion and Morality are indispensable supports. In vain would that man claim the tribute of Patriotism who would labor to subvert these great pillars of human happiness, these firmest props of the duties of Men and Citizens. ... Let us with caution indulge the supposition that morality can be maintained without religion. Whatever may be conceded to the influence of refined education on the minds of peculiar structure, reason and experience both forbid us to expect that national morality can prevail in exclusion of religious principles." **George Washington, President, United States of America**

The Lincoln Window has inscribed upon its face:

> "We here resolve that these dead shall not have died in vain. That this Nation Under God shall have a new birth of freedom. Gettysburg 1863."

Abraham Lincoln knew his Bible well, prayer and Bible study being pillars of his life and conduct. Lincoln rented his pew at the New York Avenue Presbyterian Church for $50 a year. He had a close association and deep respect for Dr. Phineas D. Gurley, pastor of the church he attended.

The Theodore Roosevelt Window has this President's thesis inscribed upon its face:

"The conservation of natural resources is the fundamental problem."

The 25th President of the United States attended church regularly. Roosevelt knew his Bible well and quoted it frequently. It was Roosevelt's belief that the Lord gave man dominion over the earth with the directive that he take good care of it.

The Woodrow Wilson Window has inscribed upon its face:

"National aspirations must be respected. People may be dominated and governed only by their own consent. Four points. 1918."

The window portrays this World War I president submitting his League of Nations proposal as an instrument of obtaining world peace. His firm faith in God, sustained and strengthened him as he was defeated by Congress in the attempt to ratify the League of Nations. Wilson's illness prevented him from attending Sunday services, much to his sorrow. His sadness was reflected in a letter written by the President to his pastor, the Rev, James R. Taylor, of the Central Presbyterian Church, on May 24, 1923. His death followed less than a year later, on February 3, 1924.

The Franklin Roosevelt Window depicts our World War II president seated in a wheelchair, with these words surrounding him:

"In the future days which we seek to make secure, we look forward to a world founded upon Four essential human freedoms."

These four freedoms were enunciated by Roosevelt in his 1941 speech to Congress. They are:

Freedom of Speech, Freedom of Worship, Freedom from Want, and Freedom from Fear.

Roosevelt, who worshipped at St. Thomas Episcopal Church, N.W., knew his Bible well. The only United States President to be elected to four terms of office, Roosevelt took each oath of office upon his family Bible, with his left hand resting upon I Corinthians 13:

" ... and now abideth faith, hope and love, but the greatest of these is love."

(Excerpted)

The Eisenhower Window has inscribed upon its face:

"I pledge allegiance to the flag of the United States of America and to the Republic for which it stands. One Nation Under God indivisible with liberty and justice for all. 1954."

It shows the 34th President of the United States, pen in hand, signing a bill to have the crucial words, *One Nation Under God* permanently grafted into our Pledge of Allegiance. Eisenhower's deep and abiding faith in Jesus Christ had been passed down to him by God-fearing parents, who were members of a group of Mennonites — the River Brethren. Both Eisenhower's pew and the *prie-dieu* at which he knelt down to be baptized by Dr. Elson can be seen in this Chapel. Prepared by Dr. Elson for his baptism, the minister said of Gen. Eisenhower:

"... he is a man of simple but deep faith, who takes his religious life very sincerely." [10]

This sincerity was evidenced by his hearty singing of hymns. Among this West Point graduate's favorite hymns were: "Holy, Holy, Holy;" "All Hail the Power of Jesus' Name;" "Faith of Our Fathers;" "What a Friend We Have in Jesus;" "How Firm a Foundation;" and "Onward Christian Soldiers." Elson recalls catching sight of the President from his pulpit in the midst of the congregational singing:

"There I saw the President, carrying probably the heaviest burden of any man in the world with his glasses on and hymnal open, earnestly singing: 'Are we weak and heavy laden, cumbered with a load of care, Precious Savior, still our Refuge, Take it to the Lord in Prayer.'"[11]

Bronze plaques on the aisle side of the pews bear the names of former Presidents, Vice Presidents and great statesmen of our nation who worshipped the Lord at this historic church. There are, on the right hand side, from the first pew down:

Richard M. Nixon, 1969-1974, The National Presbyterian Church
James Madison, 1809-1813, Pew 120, First Presbyterian Church
James Monroe, 1817-1825, Pew 110, First Presbyterian Church
John Quincy Adams, 1825-1829, Pew 134, First Presbyterian Church
Andrew Jackson, 1829-1833, Pew 81, First Presbyterian Church
James K. Polk, 1845-1849, Pew 47, First Presbyterian Church
Franklin Pierce, 1853-1857, Pew 49, First Presbyterian Church
Grover Cleveland, 1885-1889, 1893-1897, Pew 106, First Presbyterian Church
Herbert C. Hoover, 1929-1933, Covenant/First Presbyterian Church
Franklin D. Roosevelt, 1933-1945, Covenant/First Presbyterian Church
Hubert H. Humphrey, Vice President, 1965-1969, National Presbyterian Church

And on the left hand side, in the same order:

Dwight D. Eisenhower, 1953-1961, The National Presbyterian Church
Benjamin Harrison, 1889-1893, Church of the Covenant

James Buchanan, 1857 -1861, Pew 49, First Presbyterian Church
Ulysses Simpson Grant, 1869-1873, Pew 141, First Presbyterian Church
Woodrow Wilson, 1913-1921, Church of the Covenant
Harry S. Truman, 1945-1953, The National Presbyterian Church
Schuyler Colfax, Vice President 1869-1873, Pew 172, First Presbyterian Church

In the corridor adjacent to the Chapel of the Presidents, eight identical pillars express, in eloquent words of Scripture, appropriate equivalents for Science, the Arts, the Professions, Missions, Business, Education, Government and Preaching. They are as follows:

Science: To get wisdom is better than gold: to get understanding is to be chosen rather than silver. Proverbs 16:16
The Arts: The Lord made the heavens. Honor and majesty are before Him: Strength and beauty are in His sanctuary. Psalm 96:5 and 6.
The Professions:...and whoever would be first among you must be slave of all. Mark 10:44
Missions: Go therefore and make disciples of all nations, baptizing them in the name of the Father, Son and Holy Spirit. Matthew 28:19
Business: With what measure ye mete, it shall be measured to you. Mark 4:24
Education: Train up a child in the way he should go, and when he is old, he will not depart from it. Proverbs 22:6
Government: Honor all men. Love the brotherhood. Fear God. Honor the Emperor. I Peter 2:17
Preaching: Preach the Word, be urgent in and out of season, convince, rebuke, exhort, be unfailing in patience and in teaching. II Timothy 4:12

Great lessons of eternal truth can be gleaned from these columns, beneath which are names of honored members of the congregation. One of the outstanding features of the National Presbyterian Church is its stained glass windows, which diffuse the building with color and beauty. Noted master craftsman, Henry Willet of Philadelphia, originated the technique of "faceted glass" in 1954. This technique can be best described as the juxtaposition of pieces of glass an inch or more in thickness, in order to give a faceted effect, so that variegated rays of light may be diffused through them. The artist's concept of his craft is that "they are there to help create the worship but not to dominate it."

There are 42 magnificent and symbolic stained glass windows in the main sanctuary of this church. In the nave, 14 of these mirror our belief in the historicity of the Bible and our full allegiance to the Old and New Testaments. To the left-hand side (the Gospel side) of the nave, there are seven impressive windows which depict in vivid imagery, dramatic Biblical narrative: From the rear to the front, they are as follows: (1) Abraham's obedience in sacrificing his son Isaac, which is stopped by an angel of God (Genesis 22:10-14); (2) Moses' reception of the Two Tablets of the Law from Almighty God (Exodus 34:29); (3) King David of Israel holding the scroll of the Law (Psalm 119); (4) the Prophet Isaiah's speech being cleansed with a burning coal by an angel of the Lord, to prepare him for ministry (Isaiah 6); (5) John the Baptist heralding the Messianic Lamb of God, as appointed forerunner of Christ (John 1:29); (6) Stephen being stoned to death, yet pleading God's forgiveness upon his murderers (Acts 7:59,60); (7) and Paul preaching the saving Gospel of Christ on Mars Hill in Athens (Acts 17:16-34.

The seven windows on the right-hand side, (The Epistle side) reflect, from the rear to the front: (1) Noah's obedience in building the Ark (Genesis 6:12-22); (2) Joseph being elevated to the position of Pharaoh's right hand man (Genesis 41:39-44); (3) Samuel annointing David as second King of Israel (I Samuel 16:12,13); (4) A shepherd and vine-dresser, the prophet Amos (Amos 1); (5) Joseph receiving knowledge through a dream that Mary, to whom he was betrothed, was to bear a son, Jesus, the prophesied Messiah (Matthew 1:19-25); (6) the apostle James preaching the Word (Acts 15:13-29); and (7) Peter being empowered by the Holy Spirit to preach salvation through belief in Christ at Pentecost (Acts 2:14-41).

There are 16 transept stained glass windows in the main sanctuary of this church: Above each of the eight Gospel (left-hand) side transept windows is inscribed the age-old truth expressed by God's servant, Job:

"I know that my Redeemer liveth and at last will stand upon the earth" (Job 19:25).

Beneath each of these works of art, is written a truth of our Christian walk, expressed by the apostle Paul in his letter to the young Roman Church:

"... nor anything will be able to separate us from the love of God in Christ" (Romans 8:39).

The theme of these windows is the Hope of the Church as God's chosen instrument in His eternal plan and purpose for the world, depicted by the central wording:

"Behold, I make all things new."

Christ and His Bride, comprising the ransomed souls which make up His church, are depicted in this section, together with the Church Triumphant in Heaven. (Revelation 21).

The eight windows on the right-hand side of the transept show "The Church in the World Today" as their theme. Above each window are Christ's welcoming and immortal words:

"I came that they might have life and have it abundantly."

At the bottom of each is inscribed:

"You shall know the Truth and the Truth shall set you free." (John 8:32).

The Lord speaks here of abiding in His words, thereby gaining inner freedom.

The four narrow lancet windows facing the congregation on either side of the pulpit area contain excerpts from our Ten Commandments (Exodus 20); The Lord's Prayer (Matthew 5); and the Nicene Creed, formulated by the early Church Council of Nicea in the Fourth Century A.D.

The eight remaining lancet windows reiterate the pivotal doctrines of our faith based upon the Word of God and expressed through early Christian Confessions, the Continental Confessions, and several others.

The worship and praise of Almighty God is further enhanced by two fine Aeolian-Skinner organs especially built and installed for the church.

Your heart will be greatly moved by a visit to the National Presbyterian Church. Its outer and inner walls, pillars and stained glass windows express in vivid reality, the life-giving truth of God's Words. A great Monument to Prayer in the nation's capital, it exudes a peaceful serenity which infuses the visitor as he contemplates and enjoys the rich Biblical history of this country — *the one nation under God.*

Russian Orthodox Church of America

In 1918, after the Bolshevik Revolution had installed atheism in Russia, a small group of people working for the Czarist Embassy in Washington decided not to return to their own country. They began a worship community in the Nation's Capital which has, throughout the years, developed into a thriving Christian parish. Fleeing from the communist suppression of religion, a group of Russian speaking immigrants soon joined them.[12]

The National War Memorial Shrine of the Russian Orthodox Church of America was dedicated on May 19, 1963, by the Chairman of the American Battle Monuments Commission, Gen. Jacob L. Devers, U.S.A. This Church of St. Nicholas, situated on Massachusetts Avenue and Edmonds Street N.W., has served the spiritual needs of the Russian Orthodox community for over 50 years. During the first five years of its formation, the parish held services in a house at 1814 Riggs Place, N.W. The first floor served as a chapel and the second and third floors were occupied by the priest and other tenants.[13]

A beautiful iconostasis screen graces the sanctuary of this church. It comprises 26 boards, each displaying genuine Egg-Tempera Iconographic artwork. The craftsmanship is medieval in style and ornamentation. Christ "Pantocrator" or Omnipotent is the focal point on the upper portion of the screen. To His left and right respectively, stand His mother Mary and John the Baptist, while the four Evangelists look on. An ornate doorway marks the lower screen, with representations of Christ the Teacher and the Child Jesus on either side. Archangels Michael and Gabriel complete the setting.

In 1980, the church celebrated its 50th Anniversary, and many good wishes and congratulations were sent to the clergy and congregation of this communion of saints. Of the many messages, some are here quoted:

> "Thanks be to God for His many blessings;" "This is the day which the Lord hath made, we will rejoice and be glad in it. (Psalm 118);" "May your efforts in the vineyards of Almighty God be so pleasing to Him, that He will continue to shower His choicest blessings on St. Nicholas Orthodox Cathedral."

St. Sophia Greek Orthodox Church

This church stands out at the juncture of Massachusetts Avenue and 36th Street, N.W. The community of St. Sophia was founded in 1904, by a group of thirty-five newly-arrived Greek immigrant families. Services were held in various rented halls and buildings until 1919, when a church was first established.[14] The parish of St. Sophia now comprises about 4,500 souls, the foundation stone of the present building having been laid in 1951, after a large increase in membership. Built in the Byzantine architectural tradition, its mosaic and marble interior continues to be decorated and completed.[15]

The inner dome of this Cathedral gives an interpretation

of the vision of Isaiah the prophet, according to the ninth and tenth century Macedonian school of Byzantine art.[16] Intricate detail portrays the Lord of Hosts seated on His throne and surrounded by winged seraphim as described in Isaiah 6:1-3:

> I saw the Lord sitting on a throne, lofty and exalted, with the train of His robe filling the temple. Seraphim stood above Him, each having six wings; with two he covered his face; with two he covered his feet; and with two he flew. And one called out to another and said, "Holy, Holy, Holy is the Lord of Hosts, the whole earth is full of His glory."

Every major event in the New Testament is celebrated in the liturgy of the worship services of this Cathedral, which are done in Greek and English. Hymns sung during each service often reflect the gospel lesson for the day. In this Eastern Orthodox branch of Christianity, a stress is laid upon Biblical teaching through church liturgy. Icons, which can be described as "metaphorical windows to heaven," are most frequently painted upon small wooden panels. They serve as visual gospels, teaching the worshipper about the miracles of Christ, or relating symbolically the doctrines of our faith.

Symbols of the Icon: Lamps, light and flame, portrayed in an Icon, show forth the power of the resurrection, holiness, divine favor and the Word of God. Light is often portrayed as a halo. A sense of eternity is conveyed by the use of light and the absence of perspective.[17]

The crown, in icon painting is often associated with our Lord Jesus. Christ "Pantocrator," meaning Christ Omnipotent, is frequently portrayed here. Christians adhere to the New Testament doctrine that Jesus is the "crown" or fulfillment of all Jewish Law, Prophets and Writing.[18]

The deer or hart often symbolizes a faithful follower of God. These are but a few of the many symbolic teachings which Icons bring to the faithful in Eastern Orthodox Christianity.[19]

Chapter 5

Fifth Tour:
Historical Churches

Christ Church • The Church of the Presidents • New York Avenue
Presbyterian Church • Old Presbyterian Meeting House

Christ Church, Alexandria, Virginia

Founded in 1773, Christ Church served as the parish church for both George Washington and General Robert E. Lee. This thriving Episcopal church glorifies God with Sunday services, and excellent concerts. The original building, designed by architect James Wren, is Georgian in style. The interior of this lovely, historic church shows forth old-fashioned, enclosed pews which are still in use.

The engraved signatures of both Washington and Lee are found upon two silver plaques, designating the pews where these families worshipped. The visitor is startled by a unique pulpit in the shape of a wine goblet. A beautifully-calligraphied version of the Ten Commandments, the Lord's Prayer and the Apostles' Creed stands out behind the altar. This is a lovely setting in which to worship the Lord. The surrounding cemetery displays 18th and 19th century weathered tombstones, some marking the gravesite of Confederate soldiers of the Civil War. Whilst visiting the nation's capital, don't miss Christ Church — you will leave a little richer and happier for having bathed your eyes in its inspiring 18th century sanctuary.

91

The Church of the Presidents

The Church of the Presidents

Across from the White House on "H" Street, N.W., stands St. John's Church on Lafayette Square. Designed in the Greek Revival style by Benjamin Henry Latrobe, one of the architects of the Capitol and foremost architect of his time, this regal little church with its two gilded domes shining in the sun, began its long career of worship services on October 27, 1816. Since its inception, every President of the United States has worshipped the Lord here, some on a more regular basis than others. President Chester Arthur met his wife in this setting. An intimate friend of Dolley Madison, she was a member of the church, and sang in its choir. Here they were married on October 25, 1859, by the Reverend Dr. Pyne, Rector of St. John's.[1] After her death, President Arthur gave a beautiful stained glass window entitled "The Resurrection Window" to the church, in loving memory of his wife, Ellen Lewis Herndon Arthur. It faces Lafayette Square and the White House north windows.[2]

Everything within St. John's extols the beauty and glory of God, from its graceful ceilings above to the symbolic windows which capture great truths of our Christian faith. Above the main altar, a stained glass window shows Christ and his apostles partaking in their last supper together before His crucifixion and triumphant resurrection from the dead. It was designed by Madame Veuve Lorin, curator of stained glass windows at Chartres Cathedral, France.

St. John's Orphanage

Toward the close of the Civil War, the church Orphanage Association of St. John's Parish sprang up through the loving efforts of St. John's Guild. A ruling of the Guild advised young women that: "One hour every day shall be devoted to the Lord ..."[3]

The original name of the orphanage was "St. John's Hospital for Children." It began with a small rented house on Pennsylvania Avenue, in November 1870.[4] The ten beds were promptly filled. A group of five sisters, known as the "Sisterhood of St. John," soon came into being. Among these, was Sarah Williams Huntington, affectionately known as "Sister Sarah," who welcomed the poor, sad, rejected and unwanted with open arms. Sister Sarah's mode of operation was "simple living and high thinking."[5]

Records of the early years of this magnificent work of God are non-existent, Sister Sarah having dispensed with "her" children's histories for fear that they would jeopardize otherwise promising futures.

A letter and accompanying photograph of the orphans, however, was presented to the President of the Ladies Guild by Mr. Irving M. Grey, alumnus of the orphanage, in 1942. He states that many of the children "made good" in life, one of the boys becoming the Rector of a church in North Carolina. "For this," continues the letter, "so many of us are mighty thankful."[6]

The following excerpted report by Sister Sarah gives an understanding of why she was so beloved, and deeply mourned at her death in 1917:

> We might mention here another case, a most unpromising little waif, brought many years ago by the police, whom we feared to receive lest she should do more harm than receive good. The mother in jail, the most degraded of her class, what could be hoped for the child? But she seemed gradually to forget her old habits, became industrious and useful. At a suitable age she left us for a position which she filled most acceptably, spending her holidays at the orphanage; now the happy wife of an estimable farmer in her own comfortable home. We shudder to think where the little elf might have drifted, had no one held out to her a helping hand.[7]

Now at a different location in our nation's capital, and under different auspices, this ministry begun by the "Church of the Presidents" continues its work among children.

New York Avenue Presbyterian Church

The beginnings of this church can be traced to a small group of stonemasons meeting on the grounds of the White House in 1773 while it was being constructed. No less than 17 presidents have worshipped the Lord here. Historic New York Avenue Presbyterian Church is situated only two blocks from the White House. It was the result of a merger of the F Street Church and the Second Presbyterian Church, which took place in 1859. The cornerstone of the present building, a replica of the original one which stood upon this site, was laid on April 3, 1951 by President Harry Truman; its dedication taking place on December 20 of the same year. Of the United States Presidents associated with the New York Avenue Presbyterian Church, Abraham Lincoln stands out in stature and preeminence, having been a regular attendant at its services. His original dark brown pew remains at the place where he customarily worshipped, the President having been observed to always stand up for pastoral prayer. While visiting the church, do not miss the sitting room where the 16th President of the United States worshipped the Lord, together with the Lincoln Chapel which commemorates his regular attendance at the Wednesday night prayer meetings. Both these rooms have been set aside to his memory.

The Lincoln Parlor holds a precious legacy to us — the original Emancipation Document, forerunner of the Emancipation Proclamation of 1863. This document comprises three pages, penned by Lincoln himself, with a view to acquiring general freedom for the slaves. In 1953, the Reverend George M. Docherty, then minister of the church, unveiled and dedicated the document which had been presented by Mr. Barney Balaban, President of Paramount Pictures Corporation.

Another famous personage closely associated with the church was former Senate Chaplain, Dr. Peter Marshall, well respected and beloved of his congregation. He served as their pastor from 1937 to 1949. This Scottish pastor is perhaps best remembered from a book and film portrayal of his life entitled: "A Man Called Peter." Within the church, a plaque describes his impact and ministry upon those who knew him:

> "Peter Marshall made Jesus Christ a reality. He brought many of us far closer to Him than ever before."

The impressive foyer of the building contains an inscription above the padded red leather doorway:

> "The Lord is in His Holy Temple, Let all the earth keep silence before Him."

Of great significance to our nation is an historic event which took place in this church. President and Mrs. Eisenhower attended a Lincoln Day Observance Service in 1954, at which the Reverend George M. Docherty preached a sermon entitled: "One Nation Under God." The magnificence and truth of his words, reiterating the certitude of God's hand having formed and fashioned America, sparked the action which culminated in the wording "Under God" being added to our Pledge of Allegiance. This took place by Act of Congress on June 14, 1954. It was thus that Lincoln's loyal allegiance to Almighty God throughout his Presidencies was formally espoused.

Radiant stained glass windows within the sanctuary of the church portray the blessings and protection of Almighty God upon this land, together with scenes of American history and culture, as depicted within and without the Church.

The upstairs Gallery Windows carry the theme of "The Communion of Saints." They portray men and women from many different backgrounds and strata of society, who gave of their talents and gifts to form and fashion the life of the nation.[8]

They are, on the left-hand side, from the rear of the church to the front:

The One Nation Under God Window. Encaptioned beneath this historic window is God's admonition to His servant Joshua, appointed to lead His chosen people into the promised land:

Be strong and of good courage; be not afraid, neither be thou dismayed; for the Lord thy God is with thee withersoever thou goest. (from Joshua 1:9)

Among those depicted are: Jewish Americans. The Statue of "Liberty Enlightening the World" glows in the sunrise at the top of this window. She holds a torch in her right hand, while Emma Lazarus writes her famous poem inscribed upon this symbol of welcome and light to the nations:

"Give me your tired, your poor, your huddled masses yearning to breathe free ... I lift my lamp beside the golden door!"

These words epitomize what America should represent to its minorities. In the center of the window are Samuel Gompers; Revolutionary War Financier, Haym Salomon; Supreme Court Justice Louis Brandeis and Composer George Gershwin. In a lower part of this section, Broadway Producer David Belasco is featured.

Also portrayed are Indian, Spanish and Asian American men and women whose valued lives and contributions have enriched our culture and civilization. Black Americans are portrayed in a central panel. From left to right, they are: Dr. Martin Luther King, Jr., Senator Edward Brooke, Supreme Court Justice Thurgood Marshall and Jackie Robinson, first Black in major league baseball. Below these personages, is Benjamin Banneker who assisted his friend Ellicot in mapping out the ten mile square which comprised the nation's capital city in 1791.

The Handicapped of America are symbolized by Helen Keller and her lifelong companion and teacher, Anne Sullivan.

The Music Window. A window reflecting Music is encaptioned:

"He who sings prays twice."

It was given by members of the New York Avenue Presbyterian Church in grateful remembrance of those whose worship has been magnified by the sound of holy music. The window serves as a reminder to the congregation of music as a vital part of our Judeo/Christian life and heritage. The theme of this work could well be taken from the Psalms:

"O Come let us sing for joy to the Lord ... (Psalm 95:1). "Sing to the Lord a new song ... (Psalm 96:1).

The Church and State Window expresses visually an excerpt from our Bill of Rights:

"Congress shall make no law respecting an establishment of religion, or prohibiting the free exercise thereof."

Depicted along the top of this window are the three branches of our government: The Judiciary (The Supreme Court), the Legislative (The Capitol) and the Executive (The White House). Portraits of Justice Marshall, Washington, Lincoln and Jefferson stand out as representatives of this principle.

America's Laborers Window. The biblical theme of the America's Laborers window is taken from Genesis 3:19a which reads:

"By the sweat of your face you shall eat bread ..."

It commemorates the many ordinary people who have claimed the land from the wilderness, united by the rays of the cross shining in the upper left-hand corner.

The Presbyterian Church Window features in the right center, Francis Makemie, representing a milestone in the struggle for freedom of religion in the New World. It was he who, after his arrest for preaching as a dissenter, boldly declared before Lord Cornbury, then Governor of New York, that his English license to preach extended itself throughout the entire realm of the British Empire. The only minister to sign the Declaration of Independence was John Witherspoon, member of the Continental Congress. He is seen, with pen in hand, at the left center. Another great man of God is William Tennant, who founded a training school for the equipping of young men to preach and teach the Word of God, as ministers of Christ. This Presbyterian school began in a log cabin on the banks of the Neshaminy Creek in 1735. It is the famous Log College, forerunner of Princeton University, as featured in the lower center part of the window.

On the right-hand side, from the rear to the front, they are:

The Armed Forces Window, which honors those members past and present who have served and serve presently in the Armed

Forces of the United States. The lower part of this window graphically illustrates the chaos and destruction of war with the Four Horsemen of the Apocalypse as described by John in the Book of Revelation (Chapter 6, verses 2-8). A large circle encompasses the American Bald Eagle, with an olive branch in its beak and a cross over its head, symbol of the *One Nation Under God,* with Liberty, Justice and Peace for all. A globe of the world bears the word "Peace" upon it, pointing to America's peaceful intentions worldwide. Threads of connection link this orb with the four emblems of our Armed Forces: The Army, Navy, Air Force and Marine Corps.

The Lincoln Window is a magnificent portrayal of Abraham Lincoln standing in reverential awe as was his custom, during prayer at the services of the church. His original dark brown pew (the second one from the front on the right hand side), faces the altar in the same position as it did in the original church on this site. The theme of this window is Lincoln's soul-searching and humble quest for God's guidance and direction during the war-torn era of the Civil War. At the lower left is depicted Lincoln's discussions and counsels with Dr. Phineas D. Gurley, pastor at the time. A quotation excerpted from Lincoln's Second Inaugural Address validates this President's loyal commitment to our God and Father and the dedicated service rendered to his fellow Americans:

> With malice toward none
> With charity for all
> With firmness in the right
> As God gives us to see the right.

The Family and Thanksgiving Window focuses upon a congregation celebrating the Last Supper of our Lord and Savior Jesus Christ. Two thanksgivings to Almighty God for the blessings bestowed upon the land are here given: That of the first Thanksgiving celebrated by Pilgrims and Indians, and that of a present-day family thanking and praising God together.

The Education Window is an historic overview of the development and evolution of education in the United States. In the center is a little red school house and a log cabin school, resembling the one which William Tennant founded and Lincoln attended. A candle upon a Bible is the centerpiece of this window, representing the symbol of early education in America, the Bible being virtually the sole textbook. To the right of the red school house is the colonial hornbook which served to teach children without conventional books their alphabet. The window is crowned by the Cleveland Memorial Tower of Princeton University.

The Science Window commemorates Science and the Scientists of America. Many prominent scientists, mathematicians, inventors and achievers of caliber are featured here.

An Alpha and Omega, the first and last letters of the Greek alphabet, stand out in importance and preeminence in the center of a rugged cross. They may be traced to God's own words:

"'I am the Alpha and the Omega,' says the Lord God, 'who is and who was and who is to come, the Almighty.'" (Revelation 1:8)

Nine stained glass windows which enhance the beautiful sanctuary of this historic church graphically picture for us the magnificence of God's plan and purpose for His universe, beginning with the Genesis Creation (Genesis 1:1-3); then moving on to the giving of the Ten Commandments to Moses (Deuteronomy 6:4-6; Exodus 32:15 and 16); the prophets of God, Isaiah, Micah and Amos, heralding the coming Messiah (Isaiah 7:14b; Micah 6:8; and Amos 5:18 and 24); and the fulfillment of these prophecies in the birth, life, death and resurrection of the "Wonderful Counselor, Mighty God, Eternal Father, Prince of Peace" (Isaiah 53 and 9:6). The coinciding New Testament Scriptures, depicted in visual form are from Matthew, Mark, Luke, John and Acts of the Apostles. The last of these windows is the glorious Church Triumphant in Heaven. Upon the faces of the myriads of people fall the golden leaves of the tree which is for the healing of the nations. Inscribed upon the leaves, in Greek, Hebrew and Latin are the words: "Prince of Peace, King of Kings, Lamb of God," that is to say: The Annointed One, the Messiah, the Son of God, our Lord and Saviour Jesus Christ. He is shown here in the typological form of the perfect, unblemished lamb of God centered upon a cross. The Jewish Temple, with its sacrifice of a perfect, unblemished animal slain yearly for the sins of the people, is depicted in the background.

Old Presbyterian Meeting House

Built in 1774 by Scotch-Irish pioneers, the Old Presbyterian Meeting House in Alexandria, Virginia, was the site of many historic meetings and decisions in Washington's day. Today it is still a bustling church with an active membership. The tomb of the Unknown Soldier of the Revolutionary War is on these grounds and may be visited daily by the public. A plaque on the front of the building designates its unique position of importance and preeminence in the nation's history. It reads:

"May 9, 1798 having been proclaimed a Day of Fasting and Prayer by the President of the United States because of the danger of War with France, George Washington attended in this church the proclamation service preached that day by Reverend James Muir, D.D."

Chapter 6

Sixh Tour:
Early American History — Bedrock of our Freedoms

Mount Vernon, Virginia •
The National Museum of American History

Mount Vernon, Virginia

I can truly say I had rather be at Mount Vernon with a friend or two about me, than to be attended at the seat of Government by the Officers of State and the Representatives of every Power in Europe.[1]

George Washington, President, United States of America

Sixteen miles south of the nation's capital on the Virginia shore of the Potomac, lies Washington's Mount Vernon. Born on February 22, 1732 in Westmoreland County, Virginia, George Washington was the eldest son of Augustine and Mary (Ball) Washington. At age three he first came with his family to Little Hunting Creek, which was deeded to Lawrence Washington, his elder half-brother, at the death of their father in 1740. Lawrence changed the name of this estate from Little Hunting Creek to Mount Vernon, in honor of Admiral Edward Vernon, whom he greatly admired, and under whose command he served in the Caribbean Wars. Mount Vernon was George's great love, and his happiest hours were spent being a gentleman farmer on this serene riverside estate.[2]

The house itself was first built as a small, story and a half farmhouse by Augustine Washington around 1735.[3] After Lawrence's death in 1752, George leased the home from his widow.

101

Mount Vernon

At her death a few years later, the estate legally reverted to him. In 1759, he married Martha Dandridge Custis, settling his new family into Mount Vernon.[4] Martha was the widow of Daniel Parke Custis when she married for the second time. Her two small children, John and Martha Parke Custis, grew up at Mount Vernon, being quasi-adopted by her husband.[5] A good wife and mother, as well as a virtuous woman, Martha Washington read her Bible daily, meditating and praying each morning before tackling her daily tasks and responsibilities. Presently displayed in the museum which stands on the grounds of the estate, is her original, autographed Bible.[6] *(Editor's note: This has been permanently removed from public display since this chapter was completed.)*

The house is unique, being constructed of "rusticated boards," that is to say, wooden panels, to which paint is applied and to which, in turn, sand is firmly secured. The finished product resembles stone or cement, but a closer look at the exterior façade of this warm and hospitable 18th century home discloses its true identity as being constructed entirely of wood.[7] The original house was gradually extended on either side, until its present, 17-room dimensions were reached.[8]

The property comprised almost 8,000 acres, with five independently managed farms. These were maintained by 316 slaves.[9] Tobacco having been discontinued in the 1760's, wheat and cereals were the crops raised at Mount Vernon, Washington's own mill serving to grind and process his harvest for exportation as well as for home consumption. An extensive fishing industry was also carried out from this riverside estate.[10]

George Washington's serene existence on his beloved farm was interrupted by an unflinching and loyal service to his country. During the eight-year span of the American Revolution (1775-1783), he visited Mount Vernon but twice, being actively engaged as Commander-in-Chief of the Continental Army. An ensuing brief interlude, during which he enjoyed his home and plantation, was once again short-lived, as in 1789 he was elected to become first President of the United States. This necessitated the next eight years of his life to be spent primarily in New York and Philadelphia, serving his country's needs. After completing two Presidential terms of office, Washington finally retired from public life in 1797, realizing his dream of becoming the gentleman farmer and manager of his much-loved estate. In December of 1799, however, he was stricken with sudden illness and passed on from this world. According to the terms of his will, he was buried at Mount Vernon, his wife Martha joining him in 1802, a few years later.

Washington's last Will and Testament shows where his first allegiance lay: It begins: "In the name of God, Amen." Of primary concern was the liquidation of all personal debt:

Imprimus — All my debts, of which there are but few, and none of magnitude, are to be punctually and speedily paid, and the legacies, hereinafter bequeathed, are to be discharged as soon as circumstances will permit, and in the manner directed.[11]

Second on his list of importance, was the care and safekeeping of his wife, Martha:

Item—To my dearly beloved wife, Martha Washington, I give and bequeath the use, profit, and benefit of my whole estate, real and personal, for the term of her natural life ... My improved lot in the town of Alexandria, situated on Pitt and Cameron Streets, I give to her and her heirs forever; as I also do my household and kitchen furniture of every sort and kind with the liquors and groceries which may be on hand at the time of my decease, to be used and disposed of as she may think proper.[12]

Thirdly, Washington showed care and concern for his slaves:

Item—Upon the decease of my wife it is my will and desire that all the slaves whom I hold in my own right shall receive their freedom... And to my mulatto man, William, (calling himself William Lee,) I give immediate freedom, or, if he should prefer it (on account of the accidents which have befallen him, and which have rendered him incapable of walking, or of any active employment), to remain in the situation he now is, it shall be optional in him to do so: In either case, however, I allow him an annuity of thirty dollars during his natural life, which shall be independent of the victuals and clothes he has been accustomed to receive, if he chuses the last alternative; but in full with his freedom if he prefers the first; — and this I give him, as a testimony of my sense of his attachment to me, and for his faithful services during the Revolutionary War.[13]

Among prized articles at Mount Vernon is Washington's family Bible with his birth recorded therein; *The Book of Common Prayer*, bearing Martha Washington's signature;[14] a 1792 Commentary on the Book of Psalms with Martha Washington's autograph;[15] and a concordance to the Holy Scriptures, which is said to have been given by George Washington as a gift to his sister, Betty.[16] Of further interest is a letter from Washington dated July 30, 1787, to a certain Joseph Rakestraw, ordering his weathervane, which still welcomes all who visit Mount Vernon.[17]

... I should like to have a bird (in place of the Vain) with an olive branch in its mouth. The bird need not be large (for I do not expect that it will traverse with the wind and therefore may receive the real shape of a bird, with spread wings), the point of the spire not to appear above the bird. If this, that is the bird thus described, is in execution, likely to meet any difficulty, or to be attended with much expence, I should wish to be informed thereof previous to the undertaking of it...[18]

This beautiful plantation home gradually fell into disrepair and neglect. It stood sentinel on a serene hill in Virginia, overlooking the Potomac River, sad relic of heroic days gone by. Around the middle of the last century, Louisa Bird Cunningham of South Carolina cruised the river.[19] It was pointed out to her that there, on the hillside, stood George Washington's beloved home, of which he had once remarked: "No estate in United America is more pleasantly situated than Mount Vernon."

Mrs. Cunningham wrote to her daughter, Anne Pamela Cunningham, describing the state of the home. "Could not something be done about it?"[20] she asked. With a spirit of American resourcefulness and personal ingenuity which is common among our people, Miss Cunningham founded, in 1853, The Mount Vernon Ladies' Association. Two hundred acres of the original estate were purchased, and the authentic plantation home restored and refurbished to resemble the Mount Vernon of Washington's day.[21]

At the foot of Mount Vernon stands the quiet and peaceful Tomb of George and Martha Washington. On the rear wall of the tomb, above both sarcophagi, Christ's confident and matchless words ring true:

I am the Resurrection and the Life; Sayeth the Lord. He that believeth in Me, though he were dead yet shall he live. And whosoever liveth and believeth in Me shall never die. (John 11:25,26.)

National Museum of American History

This museum offers an extensive array of artifacts, items and objets d'art relating to

Lord's Prayer on a Grain of Rice —

Smithsonian Institution photo No. 80-3417

Smithsonian Institution photo No. SI-20504

The Lord's Prayer Through the Eye of a Needle —
The National Museum of American History

American culture and civilization. On permanent exhibition are the Star-Spangled Banner, Morse's telegraph, early Edison light bulbs and other famous inventions which fashioned the culture and style of life of Americans.

The Division of Graphic Arts

The Division of Graphic Arts houses some magnificent examples of microscopic engravings and printing. This is truly inspirational for those who love the Word of God. A French translation of Matthew's Gospel in book form is said to be the smallest type ever cut. It was printed from about two and a half point movable type, by Henri Didot and published in Holland in 1900. The book contains 52 pages. Six words constitute each line, with 28 lines to an inch, and 45 lines to each page. On February 10th, 1925, Alfred McEwen engraved the Lord's Prayer in a space of such microscopic dimensions that 13,500 of them would fit into one square inch. It can be seen through the eye of a sewing needle with the use of a microscope. This engraving was cut on glass by means of a diamond point and a pantograph. During the war, microscopic messages could be transmitted upon shoe nails, rings, brass buttons and the like.

The Lord's Prayer appears to have been a very popular subject in the art of microscopic engraving. A number of different examples are here exemplified, such as the Lord's Prayer engraved on 1/1,000th of a square inch; in 1/11,000th of a square inch; and upon 1/100,000th of a square inch. This was accomplished by William Webb between the years 1874-1885. On this scale, the entire Bible would occupy one-sixth of a square inch. For those who love intricate detail and precision, are three micro-engravings on paper, executed towards the middle of the 19th century. They comprise the Declaration of Independence, The Lord's Prayer and Ten Commandments. All these items can be seen only by appointment with the curator of the division in question.[22]

The Division of Textiles

The Division of Textiles affords many exquisite examples of 18th century English and early American samplers. These embroidered pieces were instrumental in preparing a young girl to function as a well-rounded Christian woman. On exhibition in the Textile Hall is a sampler executed in 1788 by 13-year-old

The Ten Commandments — 11-year-old Elizabeth Taylor's 1758 sampler

Rachel Kester of Pennsylvania. *(Editor's note: This has been removed since this chapter was completed.)* Her embroidered inscription reads:

Love the Lord
And He will be
A tender father
Unto thee[23]

The loss of treasures much
The loss of truth is more
The loss of Christ is such
As no one can restore
The lot of saints have been alway
Afflication here and scorns
And He that was best of men
Was mock and crown with thorns.[24]

Satin, cross, tent, eyelet and stem stitches were used in this work.

Another 18th century sampler was done by a ten-year-old girl, Esther Copp of Stonington, Connecticut. It reads:

Better it is to be of an humble
Spirit with the lowly than to
divide the spoil with the proud[25]

Completed in 1745, a silk-on-wool English sampler relates Psalm 37 in its entirety, commencing with an admonition against evildoers:

Fret not thyself because of evildoers
Neither be thou envious against the
workers of iniquity, for they shall
soon be cast down like the grass,
and with the green herb. Trust in
the Lord and do good, so shalt thou
dwell in the land, and verily thou
shalt be fed. Delight thyself in
the Lord, and He shall give thee the
desires of thine heart...[26]

Eleven-year-old Elizabeth Taylor's 1758 sampler displays the Ten Commandments embroidered upon two stone tablets of the law. Each tablet has a crown flanked by two lions. Vines, flowering plants and acorns surround her subject with a colourful border.[27]

Rehearsed upon many of these early American samplers is a popular format along these lines:

Katharine Mayo is my name
New England is my nation
Roxbury is my dwelling place
Christ is my salvation.
When I am dead and my bones are rotin
Here you may see my name
When I am forgotten.[28]

The sampler collection is open to public inspection by appointment with the curator of the Division of Textiles.

The National Philatelic Collection

The National Philatelic Collection comprises 15 million specimens of stamps, seals and related objects. Among this formidible acquisition of items pertaining to postage, are stamps and seals with biblical themes, quotations and personages.

The Gutenberg Bible stamp, issued in 1952, commemorates the 500th anniversary of the printing of the first book, the Holy Bible, from movable type, by Johann Gutenberg. Pictured on the stamp is Gutenberg showing his proof to the Elector of Maine.

Another famous stamp portrays George Washington taking the oath of office with right hand upon the Bible. This takes place in the Federal Building, New York City. On May 5th, 1969, a unique postage stamp was issued. It commemorates the Apollo 8 mission which first put men into orbit around the moon. Colonel Frank Borman, Captain James Lovell and Major William Anders were the astronauts on this lunar expedition. For the first time in history, the Word of God was relayed back to planet earth from the moon. A photograph taken from the moon entitled "Earthrise," is featured on this stamp. Captioned beneath the rising earth are the first four words of Genesis: "In the beginning God..." (Gen. 1:1). Under the subsection "Biblical Personages" a 1983 issue of Martin Luther commemorates the 500th anniversary of this great Reformer.

July 16, 1969 saw the 200th anniversary of the settlement of California. To commemorate this historical event, a stamp was issued. It portrays the Carmel Mission belfry, with bells joyfully pealing out the good news of eternal life through faith in Christ. Another stamp shows Washington at Valley Forge on his knees, praying. It was taken from a painting by J.C. Leyendecker. Many of the stamps are from lithographs of famous paintings displayed in the National Gallery of Art. Among these are: "The

Adoration of the Shepherds" by Giorgione, "The Annunciation," by fifteenth century Flemish painter, Jan van Eyck;" "The Small Cowper Madonna," by Raphael and "The Madonna and Child with Cherubim" by Andrea della Robbia. The 1976 Christmas issue reflects a magnificent nativity scene by John Singleton Copley. Its original can be seen in Boston's Museum of Fine Arts.

Of unusual vintage is a Christmas stamp showing the "Dove of Peace" weather vane atop Mount Vernon, home of George Washington. A dove holds an olive branch in its beak. "Peace on Earth!" the inscription reads.

The National Philatelic Collection is open to the public by special appointment only with the curator of this division.[29]

The Smithsonian Castle — The first building of the extensive Smithsonian Institution.

Chapter 7

Seventh Tour:
Reflections of His Handiwork

Freer Gallery of Art • Hirshhorn Museum and Sculpture Garden • National Air and Space Museum • National Gallery of Art • National Museum of Natural History

The Freer Gallery of Art

James Smithson was the illegitimate son of the Duke of Northumberland. He became a noted chemist who identified a variety of zinc ore which was later named "Smithsonite" after him. At his death in 1829, he bequeathed half a million dollars to the United States Government "for the increase and diffusion of knowledge among men."[1] Congress accepted the gift in 1846, and the beginnings of what has now developed into an immense complex came into being. The two rows

At the Freer Gallery — A sixth century gold cross from Cyprus

Courtesy of the Freer Gallery of Art, Smithsonian Institution Washington, D.C., (ACC. no. 10.23)

113

of buildings constituting the Smithsonian Institution on either side of the Mall, comprise the Freer Gallery of Art, the Smithsonian Castle, The Arts and Industries Building, The Hirshhorn Museum and Sculpture Garden, The National Air and Space Museum, The National Museum of Natural History and The National Museum of American History.

The Freer Gallery of Art displays one of the finest collections of Oriental art in the world. Charles Lang Freer, a Detroit businessman who made a fortune in the United States, subsequently bequeathed his entire collection of paintings, sketches, drawings, calligraphy and objets d'art to the nation. About eight percent of the gallery's twenty-six thousand items are currently on exhibition.

Taken from a London townhouse and permanently installed in the museum, the Peacock Room's Cordova leather walls were painted over with blue strutting peacocks. This was the work of American artist, James McNeill Whistler. Above the mantelpiece, in delicate pastel watercolors, Whistler's famous "Silver and Rose, Princess from the Land of Porcelain" has a place of prominence.[2]

Seen by special appointment only, the Freer Gospels comprise a valuable acquisition of manuscripts from Egypt. Treasures in this collection include: A fifth century scribal rendition of the books of Joshua and Deuteronomy on vellum, and a late fourth to early fifth century manuscript of the Four Gospels; a twelfth century Coptic Christian painting of the four evangelists on a manuscript page; leaves from eighth to thirteenth century service books of the East Christian Church; a fifth century Greek psalter; encaustic Coptic art book covers of the four evangelists; and mounted papyri fragments from the Egyptian town of Aphrodito. A thirteenth century manuscript in Armenian uncials displays elaborately decorative devices related to Byzantine painting and illumination, while a Syriac New Testament in Estrangelo script, dated 1213-1214 A.D. forms a valuable part of the collection.[3]

Striking in its originality is a mounted stone rubbing commemorating the arrival of Nestorian Christianity into China. The original eighth century monument was erected by the T'ang Dynasty of China, designating official acceptance of Christianity on their territory.[4]

Of exceptional beauty and charm is a seventeenth century Indian Deccani school painting of the Madonna and Child. The mother is clothed in a flowing Indian dress. She is seen seated under a tree, giving instruction to her infant.[5]

An object which is often on exhibition in the museum's gold treasures, is an ornate, sixth century Cypriote cross. The greek words "Phos" and "Zoe" are inscribed horizontally and vertically upon its face. These words are traced to the first chapter of John's gospel: "In Him (Christ) was life and the life was the light of men." (John 1:4).[6]

Hirshhorn Museum & Sculpture Garden

Washington's "Museum of Modern Art" had its inception on November 7, 1966, when Congress accepted Joseph Hirshhorn's gift to the nation. A site was subsequently chosen for construction of a building in which to display this collection. Gordon Bunshaft's circular stone design is constructed of reinforced concrete and is 231 feet in diameter. Philanthropist Joseph H. Hirshhorn was born in Latvia and immigrated to the United States at age six. In addition to presenting his entire collection to the nation, Hirshhorn donated a million dollars towards the construction of a building in which to house it. The ground-breaking ceremonies took place on January 8, 1969, and the dedication on October 1, 1974, at which time the museum opened its doors to the public. On that occasion, Hirshhorn's words were recorded as follows on a bronze plaque on the right hand side wall as you enter the building:

> It is an honor to have given my art collection to the people of the United States as a small repayment for what this nation has done for me and others like me who arrived here as immigrants. What I accomplished in the United States I could not have accomplished anywhere else in the world.[7]

The entire collection of art spans a period of approximately 140 years. It consists, by and large, of 20th century American paintings and sculpture. Among celebrated artists featured are Auguste Rodin, Thomas Eakins, John Singer Sargeant, Edgar Degas, Henri Matisse and Alberto Giacommetti.

John Singer Sargeant's bronze "Redemption" was executed in 1900. It depicts the dying Christ with figures of a man and woman bound to either side by a swath of material cloth, symbolizing Christ's sacrificial atonement to ransom the souls of men. Rodin's bas-relief of "The Head of John the Baptist" was finished in 1887. It portrays intense human suffering and anguish upon the face of this great saint. The third architectural model of "The Gates of Hell," was executed by Rodin in 1880. It is interesting to contemplate, and open to individual interpretation. Gargallo's rendition of John the Baptist is a contemporary work of art, on display in the Sculpture Garden. It bears the name "Prophet" and depicts the rough-hewn quality of John's wilderness existence as he heralds the advent of the Messianic Lamb. A unique portrayal of Elizabeth, cousin to the mother of Christ, was done by Jacob Epstein. She stands within the sculpture garden and appears in a homespun long dress, hands clasped attentively before her. Faith, humility and yieldedness are reflected upon her face. The name attributed to this bronze masterpiece is "The Visitation."[8]

The National Air and Space Museum

On the ground floor of this museum, one can trace 66 years of the development of aviation, from Langley's "aerodrome" in 1896 to the Lunar Module, similar to the one which landed on the moon in the 1969 Apollo 11 Expedition. Shortly after Langley's "aerodrome" came the first successful flight undertaken by Wilbur and Orville Wright's Flyer in 1903.

The first solo trans-Atlantic flight was made in 1927 by Charles Lindbergh in his "Spirit of St. Louis" Ryan aircraft. The entire flight from New York to Le Bourget airfield, Paris, lasted 33.5 hours. A periscope provided a general view of what lay ahead.

Hanging from the ceiling above are: "Glamorous Glennis," the X-1, first aircraft to fly faster than sound in 1947; and the X-15, a black, rocket-powered aircraft which represents travel at 6.7 times the speed of sound. An inside view of "Friendship 7," John Glenn's Mercury Spacecraft, is here afforded. He was the first American astronaut to orbit the globe. Then on to "Gemini 4," the vehicle from which Edward H. White made his spectacular space walk.

In July, 1969, astronauts Neil Armstrong, Edwin Aldrin and Michael Collins came back from history's first lunar expedition in "Columbia," the original Apollo 11 command module, which is on exhibition in this hall. Enter and explore Skylab's intricate and complex inner workings. The visitor is shown how the astronauts lived; how they slept, ate, and bathed during their sojourn of 28, 59 and 84 days encircling the globe. Four towering rocket-propelled missiles — Jupiter, Vanguard, Scout and Minuteman, together with a number of smaller ones, stand solemnly opposite Skylab, while a replica of the Apollo-Soyuz hook-up in space is reproduced in its entirety. A sketch gives full technical details of the orbit of both spacecraft which culminated in their successful encounter in space. An engineering model of the Lunar Rover associated with the Apollo 15 mission, together with moon rocks brought down to earth by its astronauts, are on exhibition in the "Apollo to the Moon" Gallery on the second floor. Skylab Four's command module can also be seen in this exhibition hall.

Astronaut James B. Irwin of the Apollo 15 moon landing bears witness to a supernatural encounter with the living God upon the moon. Subsequent to this experience, he gave his life for the furtherance of the gospel of Christ among men.[9] In 1973, astronaut William Pogue was one of the three crewmen on Skylab Four which set a record of 84 days in space. He says that the mission made him more firmly convinced of spiritual reality.[10] In his own words:

> "There's more to life than the body and intellect — it's the soul. There's that kernel that most of us miss."

A veteran of the longest manned voyage in space, Pogue said that he wanted a more challenging assignment. He therefore became a Christian evangelist, joining the staff of "High Flight," an evangelistic organization founded in 1972 by Irwin.[11] Irwin stated that the crew of Apollo 15 explored the moon's surface "with the power of God and Jesus Christ." "God was there," he attested:

> "The hours that I spent on the moon were the most thrilling moments of my life. Not because I was on the moon but because I could feel the presence of God. There were times when I was faced with new challenges and I asked for help. Help from God was immediate."

He further added that an experience such as his had to make man" truly appreciate the creation of God, the infinite precision with which God controls the universe."[12] Astronaut Frank Borman, who was on the first orbit to the moon in 1968, says that he saw "evidence that God lives."[13] Of further significance is a reflection made by one well acquainted with many of the astronauts, science-fiction novelist Martin Caidin:

> "There has been a tremendous change, very quietly, in the attitude and lives of the men who have gone to the moon, where they can see the planet the way God must have seen it."[14]

Dr. Paul E. Garber, first curator and now Historian Emeritus of the National Air and Space Museum, states that the Bible has the earliest printed records of man's yearning to fly. For instance, he points out that the Second book of Kings has an account of Elijah being taken up bodily out of this world in a "chariot of fire" (II Kings 2:1-11).[15] Dr. Garber quotes various Scriptures depicting men in flight, such as the prophet Isaiah's analogy: "...Those who wait for the Lord will gain new strength; they will mount up with wings like eagles..." (Isaiah 40:31).[16] The latter phrase is inscribed upon a gold medallion awarded to Wilbur and Orville Wright by Congress, upon their return from Europe in July 1909. In formulating his research, the first Curator of the National Air and Space Museum discovered that four things mystified Solomon. The first of these was "the way of an eagle in the sky." (Proverbs 30:19).[17] The writer of Proverbs describes this scene as incomprehensible and too wonderful for him. A bronze replica of the Wright medal can be seen in the "Early Flight Gallery," on the main floor of the building. *(Editor's note: Since this chapter was completed, the Wright Medallion — with its biblical inscription — has been removed from display.)*

The National Gallery of Art

On December 22, 1936, a letter from former Secretary of the Treasury Andrew Mellon was addressed to Franklin D. Roosevelt. It related the following message:

> My dear Mr. President: Over a period of many years I have been acquiring important and rare paintings and sculpture with the idea that ultimately they would become the property of the people of the United States and be made available to them in a national art gallery to be maintained in the city of Washington for the purpose of encouraging and developing a study of the fine arts... If this plan meets with your approval, I will submit a formal offer of gift stating specifically the terms thereof, and the erection of the building may proceed immediately upon the acceptance of such offer and the passage of necessary legislation by Congress... [18]
>
> Sincerely yours, **A.W. Mellon**

Mr. Roosevelt's response arrived four days later:

> My dear Mr. Mellon: When my uncle handed me your letter of December 22, I was not only completely taken by surprise, but was delighted by your very wonderful offer to the people of the United States. This was especially so because for many years I have felt the need for a national gallery of art in the Capital. Your proposed gift does more than furnish what you call a "nucleus" because I am confident that the collections you have been making are of the first rank. Furthermore, your offer of an adequate building and an endowment fund means permanence in this changing world...[19]
>
> Very sincerely yours, **Franklin D. Roosevelt.**

1948.12.1 The Return of the Prodigal Son, Bartolome Esteban Murillo; National Gallery of Art, Washington; gift of the Avalon Foundation

Return of the Prodigal Son — Among the National Gallery of Art's treasures is this painting by Bartolome Esteban Murillo.

In March of 1941, the classic, dome-shaped edifice designed by John Russell Pope was opened to the public. Its exterior facade is made up of very beautiful rose-white marble from Tennessee. Collections of the National Gallery of Art are now considered of equal importance and calibre with those of the foremost galleries in Paris, Madrid and Florence. On the main floor of the building, Galleries one through 51 encircle the West Corridor and Garden Court, spanning a vast selection of paintings from the great masters. Beginning with Florentine and Central Italian Renaissance, one moves on to Venetian and North Italian Renaissance art. These are followed by seventeenth and eighteenth century Italian paintings together with Spanish, Flemish and German acquisitions; and finally, the great masterpieces of the Dutch school of art.

Upon entering the Rotunda from the Mall entranceway, a Visitors' Center provides documentation on the location and lay-out of the building. Salvador Dali's magnificent portrayal of "The Sacrament of the Last Supper" hangs in prominence in this room. Signed and dated 1955, it represents the artist's return to Christianity, a turning point of which had been his encounter with Freud in 1938. In respect to its composition, Dali makes mention of a seventeenth century Spanish old master, Zurbaran. The devoutly-kneeling apostles, tousled heads bowed in prayer, and the precision of each fold in their ivory cloaks, show forth Zurbaran's intricate mastery of the brush. The calm waters and rugged hills seen from Dali's Catalonian home in north-eastern Spain, form a background for this otherworldly scene of blessing and security. The all-encompassing love of Christ is portrayed in His outstretched arms which form a protective covering over the entire company saints.

Gallery One

Gallery One affords paintings dated from about 1200-1350 A.D. This was a period of gradual departure from the traditional Byzantine interpretation to a more realistic form of art. Of note in this section are: The school of Cimabue's "Christ between Saint Peter and Saint James Major" which is done in three panels, the wording inscribed upon an open book reading: "I am the light of the world" (from John 8:12). The Italian master Giotto was the artist instrumental in developing Gothic painting in Italy. His painting is entitled "Madonna and Child."

Bernard Van Orley, after; National Gallery of Art, Washington; Widener Collection

The Crucifixion — This 16th Century tapestry has been permanently removed from public view

Gallery Three

Gallery Three is filled with works of Sienese artists. Among these is Duccio di Buoninsegna's "Nativity with the Prophets Isaiah and Ezekiel." The Old Testament prophets on either side of the central nativity scene foretell the first advent of the Messiah as suffering servant and Lamb of God. "The Annunciation," by Giovanni di Paolo, was painted around 1445, while scenes from the life of St. Anthony are depicted in three panels by Sassetta and his Assistant. The first panel shows St. Anthony distributing his wealth to the poor. They reflect the artist's deft eye for detail and his own perception of the rules of perspective.

Gallery Four

Gallery Four is characterized by the Florentine school of painting. The first half of the fifteenth century saw Italian artists such as Andrea del Castagno and Fra Filippo Lippi, applying the scientific principles of perspective, anatomy, and light and shade to their art. Of particular grace and beauty is Fra Angelico and Fra Filippo Lippi's world-renowned circular painting. "The Adoration of the Magi" (1445). Andrea del Castagno's "The Youthful David," painted upon a leather shield is one of the rare extant objects created for use by an old master. David is portrayed in full youth and vigour. Also of interest is Botticelli's masterful portrayal of the child Jesus and his mother, entitled: "The Virgin adoring the Child." In Benozzo Gozzoli's "The Dance of Salome" the artist has incorporated three major events which encompass the biblical narrative of Salome. In the foreground, she dances before King Herod. To the left, John the Baptist is beheaded, while in the background, his severed head is presented on a platter to Herodias, Salome's mother (from Matthew 14:1-12).

Gallery Five

Gallery Five presents us with "The Passion of our Lord" by Benvenuto di Giovanni in five panels. They are depicted as follows from left to right: 1) Christ in the Garden of Gethsemane; 2) Christ carrying His cross; 3) The Crucifixion; 4) Christ's descent into Sheol to set the souls of righteous men free; and 5) His Triumphant Resurrection from the Tomb, with Roman Centurions lying prostrate by God's power. In Giovanni's "Adoration of the Magi" one of the Three Kings is seen kissing the

Bernard Van Orley, after; National Gallery of Art, Washington; Widener Collection

The Lamentation — Also taken permanently from public view is this 85-inch by 84-inch tapestry done by Bernard van Orley

infant Jesus' heel (Gen. 3:15) Francesco di Giorgio's "God the Father surrounded by Angels and Cherubim" is fascinating to contemplate. *(Editor's note: This great master's work has been removed to storage since this chapter was completed.)*

Gallery Six

Gallery Six shows forth to the nation its only painting by Leonardo da Vinci, the world-famous "Ginevra de' Benci," painted around 1474. The portrait represents a young Florentine girl, framed against the background of a juniper tree. A Latin inscription on the back of the panel reads in translation: "Beauty adorns Virtue," descriptive of her character and attributes.

Gallery Eight

Gallery Eight has a number of interpretations which capture the interest and imagination of the viewer. They are Pietro Perugino's "Saint Jerome in the Wilderness;" Bacchiacca's "The Flagellation of Christ" and the three priceless Raphaels: "The Alba Madonna," c. 1510 "The Cowper Madonna" and "The Small Cowper Madonna."

The Alba Madonna painting is circular in shape and depicts the Son of God as an infant taking instruction at His mother's knee. His eyes, however, are fixed upon a rough wooden cross held up by the infant John the Baptist, forerunner and herald of His advent, symbolizing the purpose for which He was born into the world.

In Gallery Nine

In Gallery Nine, Sodoma's "Madonna and Child with the Infant Saint John," portrays a family grouping consisting of Mary, chosen vessel in God's plan of salvation, His son Jesus, together with John the Baptist.

In Gallery Ten

Gallery Ten provides us with Andrea del Sarto's "Charity" painted shortly before 1530. This artist followed the footsteps of former great masters, namely Leonardo da Vinci, Raphael and Michelangelo, by becoming Florence's master of the High Renaissance. Commissioned for King Francis I of France, it was, however, never delivered. The Holy Family was the artist's original theme for this work.

"Madonna and Child with Saint Elizabeth and Saint John the Baptist," was painted by Jacopino del Conte (c. 1535) and is of the Italian School.

Gallery Nineteen

Various biblical themes and narratives are immortalized on canvas in Gallery Nineteen. Among these are Borgognone's "The Resurrection" about 1510, Andrea Solario's "Pieta," and Vincenzo Foppa's "St. Anthony of Padua" of the Lombard School of painting. St. Anthony holds a leatherclad Bible in his left hand and an Easter Lilly in his right hand, symbol of the glorious Resurrection of our Lord and Saviour Jesus Christ.

Gallery Twenty

Gallery Twenty gives us a vivid recollection of "The Flight into Egypt" by Vittore Carpaccio. Here we see Joseph, Mary and the child Jesus fleeing Herod's decree to annihilate the Messiah, God's Son. (Matthew 2:13-15).

Gallery Twenty-Two

Most of the pictures in Gallery Twenty-Two were painted in Venice by Tiziano Vecellio, known as Titian, between the years 1508 and 1560. Titian's oils on canvas were painted in a number of successive layers, producing depth and luminosity which was to have an effect on European painting for centuries to come. Replete with emotion is Titian's portrayal of "Saint John the Evangelist on Patmos." Everything in this work points to John's ecstatic vision, revealed to him by Divine revelation. He is told to write this down for posterity. The book featured to the left of the saint represents the last book of the New Testament, "The Revelation of Jesus Christ ... communicated by His angel to His bond-servant John..."

Gallery Twenty-Three

Gallery 23: Jacopo Tintoretto's magnificent rendition of "Christ at the Sea of Galilee" is not to be missed. It portrays the gospel account of Jesus walking upon the waters of the Lake of Galilee, beckoning Peter to do likewise.

Gallery Twenty-Four

Gallery Twenty-Four gives a vivid interpretation of the Old Testament prophet Elijah being fed by a raven. While this dejected prophet of God reflects his total dependence upon God for his sustenance, to the left hand side above his head is God's future plan for Elijah as he departs this world in a flaming chariot of fire. The work was done by Giovanni Girolamo Savoldo.

Gallery Twenty-Seven

Gallery Twenty-seven shows Paris Bordone's masterpiece: "The Baptism of Christ" in the Jordan by John the Baptist, which is of the Venetian School.

Gallery Twenty-Eight

Moving on to Spanish masterpieces, El Greco's "Christ Cleansing the Temple" is alive with righteous anger, as He overturns the tables of the moneychangers and commercants, whipping them out of the Temple. Of further interest is El Greco's "The Holy Family." His magnificent "St. Jerome," "Madonna and Child," and "St. Martin and the Beggar" are all of exquisite beauty and biblical significance. *(Editor's Note: These three masterpieces have been permanently removed from public view since this chapter was completed.)*

Gallery Thirty-Four

Gallery Thirty-Four has a remarkable painting of "The Last Supper" by Italian artist, Sebastiano Ricci of the Venetian School (1669-1734). Of the same school is Giovanni Battista Piazetta's unusual portrayal of the Old Testament prophet, Elija, taken up in a chariot of fire. One cannot help being moved by Domenico Fetti's "The Veil of Veronica," painted about 1615. The image upon the cloth reflects the bloodstained and thorn-encrusted face of Christ as He stooped to use the veil presented to Him on the road to Golgotha. This work of art comes from the Roman School, representing a realistic interpretation of the intense suffering which the Son of God underwent to salvage the souls of those who would believe in Him. Also of interest is another great master's portrayal of the early church father, Jerome, translating the earliest Old and New Testament manuscripts into the common language of the people — Latin. Hence the Vulgate Latin version of the Holy Bible. The painting is entitled: "St. Jerome and the Angel." This work was executed by Simon Vouet of the French School. Francesco Albani's "God the Father" (1650) is also in this gallery.

Gallery Thirty-Six

Gallery Thirty-Six. An exceptional painting of the Spanish school is Bartolome Esteban Murillo's "The Return of the Prodigal Son." A visit to the National Gallery would be incomplete and lacking without absorbing the depth of compassion and love bestowed by a father upon his wayward son, as he kneels before him in abject sorrow for his wasted years. Christ's magnificent parable, recounted in Luke 15, comes to life, as one visualizes the great love and mercy bestowed upon each penitent soul who turns to God. These seventeenth century paintings constitute Spain's Golden age in culture and art, when the country was ruled by the Habsburg monarchs, Philip III; Philip IV and Charles II.

Galleries Thirty-Nine and Forty

Galleries Thirty-Nine and Forty display great Flemish works of the fifteenth century, a time when a significant school of art flourished in the Netherlands. In Gallery 39, contemplation of "The Nativity" by Petrus Christus, discloses the artist's ability to weave in biblical accounts of the Fall of Man and the story of Cain and Abel. They are, from left to right respectively, the first and fourth scenes in the archway. This he does to demonstrate man's fallen nature and his need of a Redeemer. Jan Van Eyck was court painter to the Duke of Burgundy. His "Annunciation" is filled with sacred symbolism. The elaborate tiles in the foreground of the painting depict scenes from the Old Testament accounts of Samson and Delilha and David and Goliath. The artist has inscribed Mary's words to the angel upside down and backwards, symbolizing the fact that God the Father, whose image is represented in the lancet above, may read it. This work comes from the Flemish School. For those who love rich colors and intricate detail, "Madonna and Child with Saints in the Enclosed Garden" by a follower of Robert Campin (Netherlandish, 15th Century); is of great beauty and biblical symbolism.

Gallery Forty

Gallery Forty. Of Hispano-Flemish origin, Juan de Flandes' "The Adoration of the Magi" was painted about 1510. It depicts the Epiphany as related in the second chapter of Matthew's account. The three gifts offered to the King of the Jews were gold, frankincense and myrrh. Symbolically, they depict Christ's kingship, His divinity and His mortality. Of equal beauty and importance is the same artist's "Nativity," and his "The Annunciation," in which a gentle dove, symbol of the Third Person of the Trinity, the Blessed Holy Spirit, is seen hovering above Mary as she receives God's words through the Angel Gabriel.

Gallery Forty-One

A moving rendition of "The Healing of the Paralytic" in Christ's Gospel account is attributed to the Netherlandish School (c 1560/1590).

Gallery Forty-Five

Gallery Forty-Five shows forth another Flemish artist's knowledge and love of the Old Testament Scriptures. Peter Paul Rubens has immortalized, on canvas, "Daniel in the Lions' Den" and "The Meeting of Abraham and Melchizedek." The former, which takes up most of one wall, is a world-renowned work of art, portraying God's servant Daniel, surrounded by nine ferocious lions. The prophet, however, keeps his gaze steadily fixed upon Jehovah God, his deliverer.

Gallery Forty-Six

Gallery Forty-Six presents the visitor with an interesting account of "The Levite at Gibeah" painted by Dutch artist Gerbrandt van den Eeckhout (c. 1658).

Gallery Forty-Seven

Our contemplation and enjoyment of Judeo-Christian themes in painting ends with Rembrandt van Rijn's unmatched style and mastery of the art of light and shade. Two of his works here reflect the biblical narrative. The first is the artist's interpretation of the Apostle Paul, as he struggles to write words of encouragement and exhortation to the first Christian churches, established by this "Apostle to the Gentiles," chosen by Christ Himself (Galatians 1) to spread the good news of Eternal life. The second is "The Circumcision" (Dutch School — 1606-1669), portraying Christ's circumcision on the eighth day following his birth. *(Editor's Note: Permanently removed since this chapter was completed.)*

Gallery Forty-Eight

Gallery Forty-Eight gives us Rembrandt van Rijn's heart-rending interpretation of the Christlike Joseph being accused by Potiphar's wife (unjustly and unfairly), as graphically described in the Genesis account (Gen. 39).

Sculpture and Decorative Arts

Access to these collections is gained through the Seventh Street Entrance to the building. Two magnificent sixteenth century Flemish tapestries stand out in the central lobby. They were designed by Bernaert van Orley and woven in wool, silk, gold and silver by Pieter van Pannemaker the Elder. "The Crucifixion" *(Editor's Note: Hung in the foyer in 1944, this work was permanently removed on December 11, 1987)* portrays the crucified Christ with two thieves, one on either side. The two deaths are contrasted: One dying in anguish but suppliant; whereas the other experiences a tortured and twisted death. "The Garden of Gethsemane" *(Editor's Note: Hung in the foyer in 1944, this work was permanently removed on December 11, 1987)* depicts a central figure of Christ kneeling in earnest prayer to His father. His sleeping disciples depicted in the foreground betray the shallowness of human commitment. An angel appears in a circle above, chalice in hand, symbolizing the cup of suffering which the savior of the world was to drain. *(Editor's Note: Since this chapter was completed, these two priceless tapestries, radiating the value and significance of our American Christian heritage in the Nation's Art Gallery, have been removed to storage.)*

Gallery GN1

Gallery GN1, to the left of the Central Lobby, presents the visitor with Tournai's woven interpretation of "The Raising of Tabitha." The theme of this fifteenth century Flemish masterpiece was taken from Acts of the Apostles, chapter 9. Inscribed upon an open banner, a french translation reads: "How, at Joppa, Saint Peter raised from the dead Tabitha, a good charitable women." Four widows display handsome new clothes made for them by this virtuous woman. The exquisite textile was presented by Guillaume de Hellande to the Cathedral of Beauvais in 1460. An early sixteenth century Flemish tapestry depicts Christ and the Woman taken in Adultery. Beneath the kneeling adulteress is a Latin quotation from John's gospel, chapter eight: "He that is without sin, let him cast the first stone." Consternation and shame are reflected upon the faces of her accusers, as their arms drop to their sides. The tapestry is a work of intricate detail and life-like human expression. "The Triumph of Christ" or "The Mazarin Tapestry," as it is also called, is another sixteenth century Flemish masterpiece. Composed of twenty-two warps to the inch, it is considered to be the best extant specimen of its kind from the Middle Ages. The name is derived from Cardinal Mazarin, seventeenth century Prime Minister and virtual ruler of France. *(Editor's Note: Removed since completion of this chapter, "The Triumph of Christ" was hung in GN1 in 1966, but put into storage on December 9, 1987, according to the Office of the Registrar, National Gallery of Art. It was replaced by "The Prince of Malice" Flemish, c. 1480.)*

The great central theme of Christ in Majesty upon His throne, traces its origin to the Book of Revelation. To the right is the story of Jewish Queen Esther, bride of King Ahasuerus, ruler of the Persian Empire. The Old Testament narrative is reenacted in many scenes, depicting the vital role which Esther played in delivering the Hebrews from annihilation. Two other sixteenth century works of art are entitled: "The Procession to Calvary" and "The Lamentation." *(Editor's Note: Hung in GN1 in 1974, but permanently removed to storage on December 9, 1987, since completion of this chapter).*

The latter was woven by Pieter van Pannemaker the Elder, and designed by the principle Renaissance artist in Brussels, Bernaert van Orley. The artist's garlanded border is of exceptional grace and beauty.

Galleries GN4 through GN10

Galleries GN4 through GN10 display one of the world's greatest collections of Renaissance small bronze sculpture. The collection was begun and assembled over many years by French collector, Gustave Dreyfus (1837-1914). The 1,300-item collection dated from the 15th to the 18th century, was acquired by the Kress Foundation in 1945. Of these, many portray biblical themes. Italian artist Francesco di Giorgio's "St. John the Baptist," "St. Sebastian" and "St. Jerome" were all executed in the second half of the fifteenth century. A splendid sixteenth century Milanese marble bas-relief depicts Christ as "The Man of

Sorrows," (GN6) while Bartolommeo de Sperandio Savelli's "The Flagellation" is dated 1480.

Of intricate detail are Riccio's early sixteenth century plaquettes of the Entombment of Christ. His largest single bas-relief is represented in a signed work which can be admired on the north wall of Gallery GN7. It is entitled "The Entombment."

German and Netherlandish sixteenth century plaquettes vividly display many biblical themes. Among these are the Angel Gabriel, Christ crowned with thorns; Hagar and the Angel, and the Burial of Sarah.

A magnificent Italian liturgical cross carved from rock crystals, is displayed in Gallery GN10. This work is of Milanese craftsmanship and dates to the late Renaissance period.

GN11

GN11 affords the visitor three rare bronze masterpieces. They are: Pietro Tacca's "The Pistoia Crucifix," executed before 1616, Vicenzo Dante's "The Descent From the Cross" (c. 1560), and Allessandro Algardi's "The Rest on the Flight into Egypt" (c. 1635).

GN15

On the opposite side of the ground floor Main Lobby (GN15) are the National Gallery's collections of Prints and Drawings. There are many items of significance in terms of Old and New Testament themes, such as "An Architectural Design with Christ given Over to the People," *(Editor's Note: Removed since completion of this chapter)* by Guiseppe Galli da Bibiena. This work was done with pen and brown ink, gray and brown wash. Luca Cambiaso's "Cain and Abel" *(Editor's Note: Removed since completion of this chapter)* and Annibale Carracci's "Mary Magdalene at Prayer" are both of great depth and value.

Drawings of German origin are Hans Balding Grien's "The Lamentation" *(Editor's Note: Permanently removed since the completion of this chapter)* and a late 15th Century work, "The Crucifixion." *(Editor's Note: Also permanently removed since the completion of this chapter.)* A dramatic representation of "The Parable of the Publican and the Pharisee," taken from Luke 18:9-14, was done by Rembrandt van Rijn. Here we see Christ's true illustration of righteousness versus sin. *(Editor's Note: Per-*

King Jotham's Gold Ring — From the National Museum of Natural History, this signet ring is attributed to the monarch mentioned in II Chronicles 26:2 who "built Elath and restored it to Judah."

manently removed since the completion of this chapter) Interesting to contemplate is Rembrandt van Rijn's "Christ Crucified Between Two Thieves," executed in 1653.

National Museum of Natural History

At Tenth Street and Constitution Avenue, The National Museum of Natural History was completed in 1911 and comprises more than 600 million items in its collection. On exhibition are innumerable specimens of mammals, birds, amphibians, reptiles, insects and marine life; together with a wide spectrum of gems, meteorites, geology and archaeological discoveries.

In the latter category, King Jotham of Judah's signet ring can be seen by appointment only with the curator of this division. The ring is attributed to Jotham, son of Judean King Uzziah who "built Elath and restored it to Judah" (II Chron. 26:2). The seal indicates Jotham's function as an official of Elath whose approval was needed on various economic transactions. The ring was discovered on the third level of Tell-el-Kheleifeh in the Negev Desert. Five successive settlements were found there by archaeologist Nelson Glueck. Of these, the two earliest have been identified as the port city of Ezion Geber, from which King Solomon was able to control both land and sea routes south toward Arabia and the overland route to the North; the third and fourth as the Biblical city of Elath; and the remaining one, as a 500-300 B.C. trading settlement.

Chapter 8

Eighth Tour:
Treasures from Israel & Byzantia

Dumbarton Oaks •
The Franciscan Monastery

Dumbarton Oaks

Dumbarton Oaks is well-known for its exquisite Byzantine and Pre-Columbian Art Collections, its libraries and formal landscaped gardens. Situated at 32nd and "R" Streets, North West, the name "Dumbarton Oaks" is derived from two sources: The Rock of Dumbarton in Scotland, and the original old oak trees, some of which still stand. This federal-style nineteenth century mansion was originally built for William Hammond Dorsey in 1800. A gracious, red-brick home with surrounding gardens, it became the property of Mr. and Mrs. Robert Woods Bliss in 1920. In order that a library and private collection could be accomodated, extensive remodelling and interior renovations took place at that time.

In the year 1940, some sixteen acres, to include ten acres of formal gardens, were conveyed to Harvard University, which now administers the Dumbarton Oaks Research Library and Collection.

Constantinople being the capital of the Byzantine or East Roman Empire between the years 326 and 1453 A.D., the Bliss Byzantine Collection of Art dates predominantly to this period of time, displaying many priceless treasures in its permanent col-

133

Courtesy of the Byzantine Collection, Acc. no. 47.24, (c)1985
Dumbarton Oaks, Trustees of Harvard University, Washington, D.C. 20007

Forty Martyrs of Sebaste — From the Dumbarton Oaks collection, this 14th century Byzantine mosaic icon shows 40 Christians who died rather than renounce their faith.

lection of Christian art.[1] Among these, fourteenth century miniature mosaic icons entitled "The Forty Martyrs of Sebaste" and "St. John Chrysostom" are of particular interest. A handsome copper paten with the Archangel Michael upon it dates to the 10th or 11th century, while ivory bas-relief plaques of "The Descent from the Cross" and "The Incredulity of St. Thomas" both trace their origins to 10th century Constantinople. Also to be admired is a 7th century gold plaque with the baptism of Christ featured upon it. On permanent display, "The Sion Silver Treasure" consists of sixth century ecclesiastical silver of rare beauty and craftsmanship. Control marks stamped upon many objects in the treasure indicate that they were made in a workshop in Constantinople during the reign of Emperor Justinian. Also noteworthy, is an excerpt from the lectionary of Empress Catherine Comnena of Constantinople. An ivory plaque dating back to the 7th or 8th century A.D. portrays the birth of our Lord and Saviour Jesus Christ. Two magnificent pairs of 6th century precious metal bookcovers are prominently displayed next to the Sion silver treasure. Because of the sanctity and preciousness of the Gospels, they were frequently covered with elaborately ornate bookcovers. The larger set was probably used for the four Gospels relating Christ's life and ministry on earth and therefore of utmost importance in church services. The smaller pair would most probably have been used for the Apostle Paul's letters or Epistles to the early churches which he had planted and was nurturing in the faith.

A recently acquired, late 13th century A.D. Macedonian icon of St. Peter, is exhibited in one of the museum's corridors. It is a masterful characterization of Peter, first among the apostles of Christ.

The splendid interior of the Music Room displays a painted wooden ceiling, replica of "La Salle des Gardes" in sixteenth century Chateau de Cheverny in the Vallèe de la Loire. The oak parquet floor dates to the 18th century. Original French, Italian and Spanish works of art are here exhibited. Paintings with biblical themes comprise a seventeenth century work by El Greco entitled, "The Visitation," and "St. Peter, Martyr," which was executed by Italian artist Jacobello del Fiore in the early fifteenth century. Flemish and German tapestries grace the tastefully decorated walls of this Music Room. One of these, "Christ and the Virgin" is of sixteenth century Flemish provenance, while "The Finding of the True Cross" is an original German work completed in 1480.

Outside, to the left of the main entranceway, on a large stone tablet inserted into the brick wall, you may read of the origins and stewardship of this establishment, as follows:

The Dumbarton Oaks Research Library and Collection has been assembled and conveyed to Harvard University by Mildred and Robert Woods Bliss that the continuity of scholarship in the Byzantine and Mediaeval Humanities may remain unbroken to clarify an everchanging present and to inform the future with wisdom. MCMXL.

The above is but a glimpse of what lies ahead for those who wish to explore further one of America's truly outstanding collections of Byzantine Art, together with the charm and beauty of Dumbarton Oaks.

The Franciscan Monastery

The Franciscan Monastery is reminiscent of the old monasteries in Europe. A visit to the "Church of the Holy Land in America" as it is called, is a unique and unforgettable experience. This is not only a trip to the Holy Land, the monastery having been founded by Father Godfrey Schilling in 1898 as a Commissariat of the Holy Land for the United States; but also a visit to Rome, the architecture and surrounding landscape being decidedly Italian in character and design. Part of your tour will comprise a walk through reconstituted early Roman catacombs, where first century Christians worshipped Christ in secret, their very lives being threatened. You will have the privilege of seeing the only reproduction of these early Christian hiding places in America.[2]

The Franciscan Monastery reflects Byzantine architecture, simplified to adhere to the simplicity of the Franciscan order. It is designed in the form of a five-fold cross — the one used in the Holy Land. The purpose and function of this monastery is to support and maintain Holy Places in Israel; to support churches, missions and schools in Jordan, Israel, Egypt, Syria, Lebanon and Cyprus; and to educate missionaries for those far-off fields of service.[3]

Etched upon the double-arched stone entrance to the monastery, these beautiful words greet all who enter therein:

Hosanna in the Highest! Blessed is He who cometh in the Name of the Lord. (Matthew 21:9)

These words of welcome greeted the Lord Jesus Christ as he entered Jerusalem, shortly before His mock trial, crucifixion and glorious resurrection. They originally come from Psalm

118:26, and were adapted to music by King David of Israel, in thanksgiving for God's saving grace.

The order of Franciscan Friars traces its beginnings to the year 1209. Its founder, Francis of Assisi (1181-1226) was a wealthy, successful and witty young aristocrat, whose main interests in life revolved around clothes and the acquisition of fame as a soldier. Two grave illnesses, however, turned his interests to spiritual things, and it was after finding in the gospels that Christ's disciples had no earthly possessions that he was moved to relinquish all worldly goods in his quest for spiritual treasure.

He thereupon donned a coarse tunic made of brown wool, knotted a rope around his waist and spent the remainder of his life preaching the gospel of repentence and forgiveness of sins through Christ's atoning sacrifice.

Although the Franciscans take vows of chastity, poverty and obedience, theirs is a joyful order, filled with the simplicity and love of the Lord Jesus.

This monastery is rich in Biblical themes and the reproduction of many sacred shrines of worship in Jerusalem, Nazareth and Bethlehem. The buildings are constructed in the form of five latin crosses, known as the Crusader's Cross. One central cross predominates, while four smaller ones in each angle completes the design. Among the shrines represented are the exact replicas of the Anointing Stone, The Tomb of the Holy Sepulchre in Jerusalem; the Chapel of the Annunciation in Nazareth, and the Chapel commemorating the Birth of Christ in Bethlehem. Directly opposite the Chapel of the Holy Sepulchre, at the far end of the church, is the Hill of Calvary, which one ascends, and which measures the same distance in height from the place where Christ's body was anointed for burial. The historic narrative which took place on Golgotha is vividly reenacted in a life-size plaster bas-relief depicting this earth-shaking event which permanently impacted our society. As you mount the steps, notice the Star of David, which repeats itself over and over again in the design of the wrought-iron stair railings. In the background of the relief, to the far right, you will notice the Golden Gateway to the City of Jerusalem, through which Christ entered a short week before His death. It has been closed for centuries. From this vantage point, with a turn of the head, one may contemplate the majestic portrayal of Christ's Transfiguration when His face shone like the sun and His raiment became white as lightening. At this time, He was seen on the mountain conversing with Moses and Elija by His three close friends — Peter, James and John, who had accompanied Him there. Rays of bright light diffuse the bas-relief, symbolizing God's words coming from a cloud: "This is my beloved Son in whom I am well-pleased. Listen to Him!" (Matthew 17:1-5).

In the Chapel of the Holy Ghost, a large, life-size painting shows God the Holy Spirit, in the form a gentle white dove, with shafts of dazzling light emanating therefrom. Two angels kneel in adoration on either side. This remarkable work of art depicts, to the left, Christ our Lord sending His disciples out to preach the gospel of salvation, two by two; while to the right, Francis of Assisi follows the example of His Lord as he blesses his followers and sends them out into the world.

A number of chapels within the main sanctuary graphically portray Saint Francis' conversation, life, ministry and death. This is the saint who loved animals, and who initiated the Nativity Scene, or Creche, now widely known the world over. St. Francis is purported to have received the five stigmata or wounds of Christ two years before joining his Lord.

As you explore the Catacombs, you will be thrilled to see, written upon their rough-walled surfaces, symbols of our early Christian era, such as the "fish" sign, designating the individual's affiliation to Christianity.

The landscaped gardens and Cloister Walk, with their mosaics, statues and inscriptions, should be enjoyed at leisure. Upon these grounds have been reconstituted, for American Christendom, the Chapel of the Ascension (originally erected by the Crusaders over the place of Christ's ascension on Mount Olivet); and the Grotto of Gethsemane. A gift shop within the monastery, exhibits arts and crafts beautifully fashioned in the Holy Land.

The peace and serenity of this place of prayer will go with you as you leave, having acquired a clearer perception of our early Christian church, and an appreciation for the contribution which the Holy Land has made to the United States.

Chapter 9

Ninth Tour:
20th Century National Landmarks

John F. Kennedy Center for the Performing Arts • National Headquarters of the Red Cross • Peace Monument • Union Station •
Voice of America • Organization of American States

Kennedy Center for the Performing Arts

Too often in the past, we have thought of the artist as an idler and a dillettente and of
the lover of arts as somehow sissy or effete. We have done both an injustice. The life of
the artist is, in relation to his work, stern and lonely. He has labored hard, often amid
deprivation, to perfect his skill. He has turned aside from quick success in order to strip
his vision of everything secondary or cheapening. His working life is marked by intense
application and intense discipline.[1] (John F. Kennedy, President, United States of
America)

A report submitted to the House of Representatives on Dec. 17,
1963, in conjunction with the John F. Kennedy Center Act, incorporated ideals held by the 35th President of the United States.

Nothing was more characteristic of President John F. Kennedy than his support of
the arts in America ...He believed that through its artists, its poets, musicians, painters,
dramatists — a society expressed its highest values.[2]

In 1964, a bill to establish a living national memorial to
John F. Kennedy was signed by President Johnson and passed
by Congress. It was thus that the modern, square edifice
designed by architect Edward Durrell Stone and constructed
entirely of white Carrara marble, gift of Italy, came into being.
The center opened its doors to the public on September 8,

139

Psalm 150 — Carved from rich African walnut with copper and brass lettering, sculptor Nehemiah Azaz's bas-relief covers the entire west wall of the Israeli Lounge at JFK Center.

1971, celebrating the world premiere of Leonard Bernstein's solemn "Mass."

A 45-member Board of Trustees, 30 of whom are appointed by the President of the United States for ten-year terms, sets and directs all performing arts policies. There are three main theaters on the ground floor. They comprise the Eisenhower Theater, with approximately 1,100 seats; the Opera House, seating 2,200 persons, and the Concert Hall, with a capacity for 2,700 people. The Concert Hall stage was a special gift of schoolchildren in memory of John Phillip Sousa, beloved American composer.

A Bicentennial gift to the Center from Japan, the Terrace Theater on the Roof Level of the building accomodates 500 theatergoers.

Two main entranceways lead into "The Hall of Nations" and "The Hall of States," which show forth flags in colourful array from the ceiling above. Represented here, respectively, are the 138 nations maintaining diplomatic relations with the United States; and flags of our fifty states in the Union, together with those of Puerto Rico, the Virgin Islands, Guam, American Samoa and the District of Columbia.

The red-carpeted Grand Foyer spans a length of six hundred and thirty feet, competing favorably with the Washington Monument in height. Eighteen Orrefors crystal chandeliers, each weighing a ton, dazzle the onlooker. They were a gift of Sweden. Sixty-feet tall Belgian mirrors line the inner walls, reflecting further the resplendant glitter of this Performing Arts Hallway.

In the center of the foyer, an unusual bronze rendition of Kennedy's head greets the eye. Sculptor Robert Berks has captivated the poise and life-like facial expressions of his subject. It is said that Kennedy's profile betrays a smile on the one hand, and sadness on the other.

A gift of the State of Israel, the Israeli Lounge was dedicated on November 30, 1971. No less than forty-eight musical instruments mentioned in the Old Testament are displayed upon its walls. The visitor is overwhelmed by an exciting and colourful biblical panorama. A masterpiece of both literal and symbolic interpretation, Psalms 81 and 150 orchestrate their own praises to Jehovah God through the artists' skillful expression upon wall and ceiling.[3]

Splendid royal blues and reds painted upon forty panels in the ceiling depict Shraga Weil's interpretation of Psalm 81:

The Creation — Seven large Aubusson tapestries, gift from Australia to the United States, commemorate the Seven Days of Creation and adorn the walls of JFK Center's roof level.

Sing aloud unto God our strength
Shout unto the God of Jacob
Take up the melody, and sound
the timbrel
The sweet harp with the psaltery
Blow the horn at the new moon
At the full moon for our feast-day
For it is a statute for Israel
An ordinance for the God of Jacob[4]

Portrayed upon these panels, is Joshua at the walls of Jericho, blowing a ram's horn; David playing his harp; and Miriam dancing and singing to celebrate the passage of the Israelites through the Red Sea.[5]

Carved from rich African walnut in bas-relief with copper

and brass lettering, the entire West Wall of this lounge represents sculptor Nehemiah Azaz's rendition of the last of the Psalms, which ends in joyful praises to our God and Father.

> Praise Him with trumpet sound
> Praise Him with lute and harp
> Praise Him with timbrel and dance
> Praise Him with string and pipe
> Praise Him with sounding cymbals
> Praise Him with loud, clashing cymbals[6]

Seven large Aubusson tapestries entitled "The Creation" adorn the walls on the Roof Level of the Center. A gift from Australia, they were executed by John Coburn, designer of the curtains in the new Sydney Opera House. Each tapestry has a theme of its own, taken from the first chapter of Genesis and captioned with a simple phrase by the artist himself: The first Day: The Spirit of God brooded over the waters. The Second Day: God seperated the light from the dark. The third Day: God created the Earth. The Fourth Day: God created the vault of the sky and He made the sun and the moon and the stars to shed their light on the earth. The Fifth Day: God created the fish of the sea, the birds of the air and the beasts of the dry land. The Sixth Day: God created men. The Seventh Day: God rested.[7]

Each Christmas sees Handel's majestic and awe-inspiring "Messiah" performed by the National Symphony Orchestra, with Mistislav Rostropovitch as its conductor. The Choral Arts Society adds its own compositions to this rich heritage of Christmas music glorifying Christ.

Red Cross National Headquarters

> The Red Cross is perhaps the most recognized and most welcome symbol in the world. It is a symbol of unflagging vigour and unfailing help in time of need. It is a symbol of man's abiding concern for all his brothers.[8]
> **John F. Kennedy,** President, United States of America

This impressive white marble edifice has been the national headquarters of the Red Cross since its completion in 1917. It commemorates the selfless devotion of women from the north and south who cared for the sick and dying of the Civil War. The building has been set apart as a national historic landmark. Upon entering the main lobby, do not forget to sign the guest book to the right. An interesting display cabinet to the left shows casts of the commemorative gold medal, designed at

The National Headquarters of the Red Cross

the United States Mint in Philadelphia, Pennsylvania. An inscription describes its purpose, as follows:

"This gold medal was authorized by Congress to be produced by the U.S. Mint in honor of the American Red Cross Centennial. The medal was presented on May 21, 1981 by Vice President George Bush during the Red Cross National Convention in Washington, D.C."

The medal itself has the dates 1881-1981 upon its face, with the wording: "A medal of the Congress: People helping people."

On May 21, 1881, Clara Barton founded the American Red Cross, with the first local society being established in Dansville, New York. Brochures in the foyer of this building describe the heroic lives of Henry Dumont, Dr. Charles Drew, Jane Delano and others who were instrumental in the development of this worthy and compassionate cause.

As you wind your way up the stairs to the second floor, three marble busts greet the eye. They are "Faith," "Hope" and "Charity," beautifully executed by sculptor Hiram Powers.

In the Board of Governor's Hall on the second floor, the visitor is struck by the radiant beauty of three Tiffany stained glass windows of exceptional originality and inspiration. They are a gift from the Women's Relief Corps of the North and the United Daughters of the Confederacy. The window to the left portrays St. Filomena as she sets out on an errand of ministry to the sick. Accompanying her is a young woman carrying a shield with the Red Cross emblem upon it, and four damsels who bear the names "Charity," "Mercy," "Hope," and "Faith." Each carries a special gift of her own. The central window displays a group of splendidly-attired knights riding the clouds upon bejewelled horses. One of these knights is seen giving a drink of water to his fallen comrade. Services which the Red Cross renders during the war are here depicted. The right-hand side window portrays a maiden, "Fortitude," her apron overlowing with the red roses of good deeds. A single wooden cross — the cross of Christ — is carried by the young women who leads this procession.

In the rear of the Board of Governor's Hall, the trowel used by President Woodrow Wilson in laying the cornerstone to the building on March 27, 1915, is displayed.

Renowned for his ability to recreate life-like forms from the original, sculptor Felix de Weldon's memorial to the Red Cross dead adorns the South Garden. It honors those who gave their lives to serve others and portrays three figures straining to help the fallen, symbolizing Christian love and compassion. The sculptor sees his work as representative of "people giving generously of themselves to alleviate suffering, always ready to serve with strong arms and with warmth and sympathy."

Soldiers of the First World War nicknamed the nurses of the Red Cross, "Very Adaptable Dames." A marble monument to the north of the garden walk is in memory of the founder of Red Cross Nursing and Health Services, Jane A. Delano, together with 296 Red Cross nurses who gave their lives in the service of others during the First World War. An inscription on the base of the monument is from Psalm 91:

> Thou shalt not be afraid for the terror by night; nor for the arrow that flieth by day; nor for the pestilence that walketh in the darkness; nor for the destruction that wasteth at the noonday. (Psalm 91:5-6)

The Peace Monument

Just below the West Capitol grounds, where Pennsylvania Avenue and First Street intercept, the Peace Monument attracts the attention of many visitors. It stands as a silent testimony to naval heroes of the American Civil War. Two muses represent America weeping on the shoulders of History. History holds a book in her left hand honouring these mighty men of valour. An inscription upon it reads as follows: "They died that their country might live."

Union Station

Towards the middle of the nineteenth century, the advent of the locomotive brought about a new way of life. An 1896 article written by former stagecoach driver, Charles Eliot, appeared in the Washington Evening Star. It describes a quaint, but out-moded means of travel:

> ...Every night after supper at the taverns where we stopped, they would have a royal good time. A royal blue time, they called it, for you see, they knowed nothing about painting the town red. So they came on until they got to Fredericksburg (Va.), where they cleaned themselves up, took a bath, and come into Washington, fresh as kids.[9]

In 1903, Congress passed an Act "to provide for a union rail-road in the District of Columbia and for other purposes."[10] Architect Daniel H. Burnham, who headed the 1893 World Columbian Exhibition in Chicago, was chosen as designer and architect of Union Station, completed in 1908.[11] The six statues on the front façade of this elegant white marble edifice are the work of Louis Saint-Gaudens, son of renowned American sculptor, Augustus Saint-Gaudens.[12] Each 18-foot tall granite statue weighs twenty-five tons.[13] Noble ideals confront the traveller, as he catches sight of the carefully-chosen inscriptions depicting each silhouetted muse. Charles W. Eliot, former President of Harvard University, was consulted in choosing a theme for both sculpture and inscription. Beneath the statue for "Fire and Electricity," God's words through David, King of Israel, ring true: "Thou hast put all things under his feet."[14] This quotation comes from Psalm Eight, which reflects God's glory and man's dignity. Under the statue "Freedom and Imagination," Christ's message from John 8:32 is cited: "The Truth shall Make you Free."[15] Jesus is here referring to abiding in His Words. Beneath the inscription for "Agriculture and Mechanics," the Old Testament prophetic utterance pertaining to Israel is given: "The desert shall rejoice and blossom as the rose" (Isaiah 35:1).[16]

Inscribed on the Attic wall of the State Entrance, South Elevation, are beautiful and timely words of exhortation to all who pass by:

> "Let all the Ends thou Aim'st at be Thy Country's, Thy God's and Truth's, Be Noble, and the Nobleness that lies in other men, sleeping but never dead, will rise in majesty to meet thine own."

Union Station is one of the most attractive and interesting sights in the nation's capital. The Columbus Fountain enhances its driveway with a fifteen-foot tall statue of Italian-born traveler and discoverer of the new world, Christopher Columbus. Three handsome flagpoles tower above his fountain, symbolizing Columbus' three sailing ships — the "Niña," the "Pinta" and the "Santa Maria." To the right, the Old World, with its teeming population and limited horizons is portrayed in the form of a wizened old man. The New World, with its wide open spaces and innovative ideas is seen in the figure of a young and forward-looking American Indian, to the left.

The Voice of America

In representing the United States abroad, the Voice of America serves as a reliable and authoritative source of worldwide news. Its principles incorporate an accurate and objective presentation of American thought, its institutions and policies, together with objective discussions thereon.[17] Regular broadcasts are made in forty-four languages.[18] Approximately 1200 hours of direct broadcasting is put out by V.O.A. per week, as compared with 2259 by the U.S.S.R., 1411 by China; 820 by the Arab Republic of Egypt; 821 by the Federal Republic of Germany and 737 by the United Kingdom. Twenty-two commercial circuits feed V.O.A. relay stations, which in turn beam shortwave frequencies abroad via satellite transmission.[19]

German-born Father Victor Potapov came to the United States at age two. His formal theological training was acquired at Holy Trinity Russian Orthodox Seminary in upstate New York. He has been with the Voice of America now for almost ten years, broadcasting a 45-minute predominantly Christian program in the Russian language, which is repeated six times throughout the week to the U.S.S.R., and several times weekly to Siberia.[20]

The Breakfast Show on Moscow time, transmitted throughout the Soviet Union includes a three-minute Scripture reading. Father Potapov sees this program as being of crucial importance, the Russian people lacking religious literature due to its prohibition.[21] His broadcasts include Scripture, theological texts, news of Christian life in America, an explanation of Church feast days, and the importance of the Bible. Senators and Congressmen interested in the plight of Christians persecuted in the U.S.S.R. are interviewed informally, giving their listeners the assurance of our moral support. A Vesper Service is broadcast weekly on Sundays at 1900 hours Vladivostok time. One hundred million shortwave radio sets are estimated for the U.S.S.R.[22]

Father Potapov's stress is not upon one denomination, but rather upon the things of value to all followers of Christ. Subjects in his repertoire have included: Pentecost; The Dogma of the Holy Trinity; Characterists of sainthood; The Plain People: Amish and Mennonites; Graduation at Holy Trinity Seminary; Fifty Senators ask Soviets to allow Pentecostals to Emigrate; The Emigration of Mennonites from Russia to the United States; and the Meaning of Repentance in the Christian Church.[23]

Father Potapov is particularly thrilled about the formation of "The Millenium Committee," commemorating 1,000 years of the Christianization of Russia (988-1988). The basic purpose of this committee is to encourage and promote commemorative undertakings by as many institutions as possible both in the United States and abroad. Included in the many 1988 year-long exhibits, lectures and conferences planned were: the January 17-21 Conference on the Influence of Christianity on state and society in contemporary Russia, at the Monterey Institute of International Studies in California; the January 28 conference "Soviet Union Update," on recent developments affecting church and religion, at the Interfaith Center in New York; a May 8 Gala Millenium anniversary "Rostropovich in Concert" at Riverside Church in New York City; and the June 12 official Millenium "Jubilee" in Moscow, when Patriarch Pimen will preside over the ceremony at Danilov Monastery, with many foreign guests in attendance.

According to this man of God, an upsurge of interest and curiosity in Christianity has been engendered in the Soviet Union, especially among the youth, who are asking themselves the question: "Why are there so many Biblical themes in our literature, paintings, art, architecture and sculpture if it is not important?"

On November 24, 1983, Voice of America broadcast its very first worldwide English language Thanksgiving Day Service from Boston's historic church, the Old South Meeting House. Christmas, 1983, saw numerous Christian programs broadcast in different languages abroad. Programs have included the following topics: "Jesus Christ: His birth, His Impact;" "The Custom of Carolling;" and "Christmas through the Eyes of Children."[24]

Here are some excerpts coming from these programs which

point to our Biblical roots as a nation firmly founded upon God's Word:

Olvera St., Los Angeles " 'Posada' means lodging or shelter and refers to the story told in the Bible (The Christian Holy Book) of the journey of Mary and Joseph to Bethlehem where they sought lodging before Jesus was born. The Holy family finally ended up taking refuge in a stable where Mary gave birth to the Christ child. Today, each town has its own way of depicting this story through Las Posadas ... It's a very humble ceremony. It's not a Hollywood production."[25]

Jesus Christ: His Birth, His Impact "He was born of the Virgin Mary in the city called Bethlehem in Judea, which is now Israel. And, in this birth, God became man and walked among us and He came to save us from our sins, to give us new life, to open the door to eternal life for all of us who believe in Him and to bring about reconciliation between humanity and God and the people of this earth with one another."[26]

The master control for this organization is in our nation's capital and can be toured during the five working days of the week. Live news broadcasts to countries abroad are fascinating to watch. You will carry away a lasting and memorable experience of the Voice of America's broadcasting network, and vast outreach across our globe.

The Organization of American States

President Theodore Roosevelt laid the cornerstone to this building in 1908. Three-quarters of its cost was a gift of philanthropist Andrew Carnegie. Two years later, in April, 1910, the site was dedicated as the International Headquarters of the Organization of American States. The handsome edifice, its outer facade constructed of white Georgian marble, was primarily designed to resemble a Spanish colonial mansion, but includes English, French, Portugese and American streams of architecture. The sculptured groupings to either side of the main entranceway represent South America to the left and North America to the right. The latter is a work of art executed by the sculptor of Mount Rushmore in South Dakota, Gutzon Borglum.[27]

Daniel the Prophet (the statue of)

An exact granite replica of the original stands beneath the branches of a tall evergreen tree on the front lawn. Its original stone model, executed by Brazilian sculptor Antonio Francisco Lisboa (1730-1814) stands in Ouro Preto, Brazil. He was a much-loved artist, affectionately known as "Aleijadinho," meaning, "the crippled one." Daniel stands alone — placid and calm — with a lion at his feet. To the side of the statue an inscribed scroll indicates his identity as Old Testament prophet of God, who predicted the four Great World Empires and the seven years' Great Tribulation.[28]

Isabel la Catolica (the statue of)

All who visit Washington must see the regal life-size statue of Isabella of Spain, who provided the financial means so that Christopher Columbus could accomplish his voyage of discovery to the unknown west. The statue stands sentinel directly in the foreground of the building. Spanish sculptor Jose Luis Sanchez made the bronze cast by the process of "lost wax." Its style is original and contemporary. Isabella holds a pomegranate in her hands, from which a dove, symbol of the Holy Spirit, takes flight. This extraordinary work of art, dedicated on April 14, 1966, was a gift of the Institute of Hispanic Culture in Madrid.[29]

Chapter 10

Tenth Tour:
Monuments to Great Men of God

Francis Asbury • Martin Luther •
John Wesley • John Witherspoon

Francis Asbury (the statue of)

Henry Augustus Lukeman's bronze statue of Francis Asbury, pioneer of American Methodism (1745-1816), is a most unusual one. Broad-brimmed hat pulled over his brow, the rider's facial expression betrays noble features and a mouth set firmly in unswerving purpose. Asbury's left hand holds a loose rein, while his right clasps a Bible to his breast, fingers marking a particular reading. His horse fawns the ground, denoting incertitude, which is in direct contrast to the resoluteness of his master. Engraved on the marble pedestal upon which this work of art stands, are the words:

"If you seek for the results of his labor you will find them in our Christian civilization"

and

"His continuous journeying through cities, villages and settlements from 1771 to 1816 greatly promoted patriotism, education, morality and religion in the American Republic." Act of Congress

In keeping with the lines of suffering and deprivation traced upon his countenance, Asbury's mission in life is described upon the rear of the statue as: "The Prophet of the Long Road."

151

Martin Luther (the statue of)

On the triangular promonitory between Vermont and N Street, N.W., the statue of Martin Luther (1483-1546) stands out in originality and resolute muteness. His timeless message has been conveyed to passersby since the statue's inception, commemorating Luther's 400th birthday. Cast in Germany in 1884, it is a duplicate of the original by E. Reitschell, which stands in Worms, Germany. The eleven and a half foot tall bronze replica of one of the outstanding leaders of the 16th century Reformation holds a large leather-bound volume of the Scriptures in his left hand with his right, clenched fist resting upon its contents, as if to say "This is God's Word — Go by it alone! Let it be your guide in life!"

Luther wears a long, beltless cloak draped around him. His face is set as a flint with his eyes looking straight ahead. The sculptor portrayed this great man of God in the act of oratory — of which he was a master.

John Wesley (the statue of)

Arthur George Walker is the sculptor of this moving bronze statue of John Wesley, great preacher and evangelist, who was instrumental in initiating a mighty revival in Britain and a return to biblical roots. He holds in his hand an open Bible, the source and strength of his dynamic calling and ministry. The statue distinguishes itself from other equestrian statues of great military heros in the city, all of whom exude confidence and success. On the contrary, this hatless founder of Methodism sits astride his docile and calm horse, an expression of meekness, gentleness and purpose on his face. He stretches forth his hand in a gesture of giving forth the Word of God, in obedience to Christ's Great Commission.

John Witherspoon (the statue of)

At the intersection of N and 17th Streets, N.W., this handsome and imposing bronze, ten-foot tall statue stands out as a staunch reminder of the signers of the Declaration of Independence. A Bible is firmly clasped in his right hand. Former President of the College of New Jersey at Princeton, this Scottish-born Presbyterian Minister was the only minister among the signers of the document marking the birth of a new nation. A bronze plaque on the rear pedestal of the statue reiterates a statement made by this great man of God:

For my own part, of property I have some, of reputation more. That reputation is staked, that property is pledged on the issue of this contest; and although these gray hairs must soon descend into the sepulchre, I would infinitely rather that they descend thither by the hand of the executioner than desert at this crisis the sacred cause of my country. John Witherspoon 1722-1794

The Lincoln Memorial

Chapter 11

Eleventh Tour:
America Remembers Her Fallen Sons

Lincoln Memorial • Arlington National Cemetery • Iwo Jima Memorial • The Netherlands Carillon

The Lincoln Memorial

I do, therefore, invite my fellow-citizens in every part of the United States, and also those who are sojourning in foreign lands, to set apart and observe the last Thursday in November next as a day of thanksgiving and praise to our beneficent Father who dwelleth in the heavens. (signed) A. Lincoln. October 3, 1863. Proclamation for Thanksgiving by the President of the United States.[1]

On the 28th August, 1963, Dr. Martin Luther King Jr. delivered from the steps of the Lincoln Memorial, his now famous "I have a Dream" speech to over 200,000 people. The following is an excerpt:

I have a dream that one day every valley shall be exalted, every hill and mountian shall be made low, the rough places will be made plains, and the crooked places will be made straight, and the glory of the Lord shall be revealed, and all flesh shall see it together. (from Isaiah 40:4-5)[2]

The cornerstone of the building was laid in 1915, and its dedication took place on Memorial Day, 1922. In completing this memorial, which honors the sixteenth President of the United States, Architect Henry Bacon made this observation: "...any emulation or aspiration engendered by the memorial to Lincoln and his great qualities is increased by the visual relation of the

155

Washington Monument and the Capitol."[3] Both of these edifices are seen in a perfect straight line with the Reflecting Pool from the steps of Lincoln Memorial, one of the loveliest views in Washington. Constructed to resemble the Parthenon in Athens, the thirty-six doric columns which form a colonnade around the edifice reflect the existing states in the Union at the time Lincoln was assasinated. Inscribed on the upper attic walls are names of the 48 states in existence at the time the memorial was inaugurated in 1922. Upon entering the building, a rare sight awaits the visitor. A 19-foot tall marble statue portrays the President seated in an armchair. His face is pensive and thoughtful. Sculptor Daniel Chester French spent four years carving this remarkable image of Abraham Lincoln from 28 blocks of white Georgia marble. Lincoln's expression is both powerfully introverted and drawn, indicating the intense struggle of the Civil War.

The building stands close to 80 feet tall, the central chamber measuring 74 feet in height and 60 feet in width. Bronze girders on the ceiling contain laurel and oak leaves, designed by Jules Guerin. The interior walls are constructed of Indiana limestone, while pink Tennessee marble comprises the inside floor and wall base. Each of the two handsome tripods flanking the entranceway to the doric colonnade is 11 feet tall. The Gettysburg Address is featured on the inside South Wall, while on the opposite wall, Lincoln's Second Inaugural Address takes its stance. Above each address, a symbolic mural by Jules Guerin allegorizes Lincoln's ideals and principles of conduct.

Guerin's mural on the south wall is entitled "The Emancipation of a Race." The central figure portrays the "Angel of Truth," who sets a slave free. Shackles fall from the slave's arms and feet. The grouping to the left symbolizes "Justice and Law." A sword of Justice and the scroll of the Law are held by a central figure seated in the chair of the Law. Two upright guardians of the law hold torches of Intelligence. The grouping to the right depicts "Immortality." "Faith," "Hope," and "Charity" stand by as a seated damsel receives the imperishable crown of immortality.[4]

The meaning here is that Eternal Life is acquired through faith in Christ, Hope in Christ and Love that is shed abroad in our hearts to others after the Holy Spirit indwells us at salvation.

The north wall painting typifies "Reunion." The central figure represents the Angel of Truth, who unites the North and the South by joining their hands together in a handclasp. To the left is a scene entitled: "Fraternity."[5] The central figure here is a woman who enfolds a man and a woman in her arms. This signifies the family nucleus replenishing the abundance of the earth. Vessels of wine and oil, symbols of Eternal Life, flank this grouping on either side. The right grouping shows "Charity" in predominance.[6] She is seen with her helpers, caring for orphans and administering the water of life to the lame and the blind. This is I Corinthians 13 in action. The artist used about 300 pounds of paint to execute his work, which was done on two pieces of canvas, each weighing 600 pounds. White lead and Venetian varnish were used to affix these canvases to the wall, making them entirely weatherproof. Forty-eight figures are represented in the two murals.[7]

Appropriately centered above the statue of Lincoln, in large capital letters, are engraved the words:

"In this temple as in the hearts of the people for whom he saved the Union, the memory of Abraham Lincoln is enshrined forever."

Arlington National Cemetery

Across the Potomac River in Virginia, in a direct straight line with the Lincoln Memorial, lies Arlington National Cemetery. This site was the original 1,100 acre tobacco plantation belonging to Gen. Robert E. Lee, who married Mary Anne Randolph Custis, only surviving child of George Washington Park Custis, (George Washington's adopted grandson), and Mary Lee Fitzhugh.

At the break of the Civil War, Robert E. Lee resigned from the U.S. Army, stating that he could not lift his hand against family and friends of his native Virginia. His plantation home unoccupied, Union forces soon took over the premises. A law required that all private property owners should appear in person to pay their taxes, Mrs. Lee sent a cousin to pay the taxes amounting to $97.04. The government turned it down, however, purchasing the estate on public auction shortly thereafter. It was thus that Robert E. Lee's Arlington home became a national cemetery.

Twenty years later, Custis Lee, Gen. Lee's son, took his father's last Will and Testament to the Supreme Court. The court's ruling reinstated Lee as rightful owner of this estate. Unable to live on the site of a now-established cemetery, however, Lee sold it to the U.S. government in 1883 for a hundred and fifty thousand dollars.

About 207,000 people are buried here. Only retired military or those on active duty, the wives and widows of military, children of military under 18 years of age, and the recipients of the gold Medal of Honor, the Distinguished Service Cross, the Distinguished Service Medal, the Navy Cross, the Silver Star and the Purple Heart, have the right to be buried at Arlington.

Most of the tombstones, that is, those of regular dimensions, are provided by the government. A circle upon the face of each shows forth a cross or a star of David in the vast majority of cases, designating the individual's faith at time of death.

On the day he was inaugurated into office, the 35th President of the United States spoke these words:

> And so, my fellow Americans, ask not what your country can do for you. Ask what you can do for your country. My fellow citizens of the world. Ask not what America will do for you, but what together we can do for the freedom of man. Finally, whether you are citizens of America or citizens of the world, ask of us the same high standard of strength and sacrifice which we ask of you. With a good conscience our only sure reward, with history the final judge of our deeds, let us go forth to lead the land we love, asking His blessing and His help, but knowing that here in earth God's work must truly be our own. **John F. Kennedy,** President, United States of America

Here he lies buried, on a hillside just below Gen. Lee's lovely plantation home, overlooking the capital city which he admired. The site of Kennedy's tomb, executed by architect John Warnecke, exemplifies simplicity and pureness of design. A central plaque designates Kennedy's dates of birth and death. The eternal flame, unique to all our military cemeteries across the land, stands guard at his graveside. To the right and left of Kennedy's tomb are plaques for his still-born daughter, and his son, Patrick Bouvier Kennedy, respectively. The latter child lived only two days, dying but a few months before his father's assasination. Famous excerpts from Kennedy's Inaugural Address are engraved upon a semi-circular wall directly facing his tomb.

Adjacent to John Kennedy's tomb is the simple grave of his brother Robert. A plain wooden cross is what he desired. It is painted white. A white marble plaque bears his name, date of birth and death. A shallow, rectangular pool of water symbolizes eternal life through the atonement of Christ, while the inscriptions above it are two famous human rights speeches made by Robert Kennedy. The first was delivered in South Africa, in 1966, and the second in Indianapolis, Indiana, in 1968.

A glance towards the Robert E. Lee mansion, shows a U.S. flag flying high. This flag is lowered to half mast just before the first funeral of the day, and hoisted back to its normal height following the last funeral each afternoon. An estimated 20-25 funerals occur daily. To the left of the flagpole is a handsome marble sarcophagus with a flat, table-like top. It represents Pierre Charles l'Enfant's tomb and overlooks the spectacular city which he designed almost 200 years ago. This talented engineer died impoverished in 1825 at the home of his friends, the Digges family of Maryland. He was buried in an obscure and unmarked grave at "Green Hill," the farm belonging to William Dudley Digges. Towards the turn of the century, however, the American people realized the enormous debt of gratitude owed this great Frenchman who had conceived and executed the plans for their capital city. In 1909, his mortal remains were disinterred, his body lying in state in the Capitol and honoured by the President of the United States. Shortly thereafter he was given the posthumous honour of being buried in Arlington National Cemetery, overlooking the beautiful city which he had designed.

A rather steep walk up the slope leads to the Tomb of the Unknown soldier. The sacred burial place of the unknown soldier of the First World War is designated by a 72-ton block of white marble, upon which this inscription reads:

Here lies in Honoured glory, An American soldier known but to God.

In front of the Tomb are plaques designating the unknowns of the Second World War, the Vietnam War and the Korean War, respectively.

The changing of the Old Guard (Third United States Infantry and official Presidential unit) takes place every hour on the hour during the winter months. In the summer months, the guard changes each half hour. Throughout the year during nighttime hours, the guard changes every two hours. A thorough inspection of the on-coming guard is made by the Relief Commander. The permanent marching watch of this Honour Guard demonstrates duty to God and country, performed with pride and dignity.[8]

The Iwo Jima Marine Corps Memorial

"Uncommon valor was a common virtue." Admiral Chester Nimitz

The above tribute was first expressed in a communiqué from Iwo Jima, applauding our servicemen as they battled cease-

The Iwo Jima Memorial

lessly to attain control of this strategic Japanese island. Seven hundred and fifty miles south of Tokyo, Iwo Jima became the symbol of courage and sacrifice to the American people.

On February 19, 1945, a force of approximately 71,245 men, 66,953 of them Marines, waited off the coast of this island which had been bombed and shelled 72 consecutive hours prior to their arrival. For 25 days the battle raged. The final toll was a heavy one: 5,885 marines lost their lives, and a further 17,272 were injured, demonstrating the high price of liberty. A few days after the landing, five Marines, together with a Navy Corpsman, climbed laboriously to the top of Mount Suribachi with an iron pipe, to which had been attached the American flag. Their names are as follows: Private First Class Franklin Runyon Sousley; Corporal Ira Hamilton Hayes; Sergeant Michael Strank; Corporal Rene Arthur Gagnon, Corporal Harlon Henry Block and Pharmacist's Mate Second Class John Henry Bradley. The star-spangled banner was firmly emplanted into the grit and grime of Mount Suribachi's volcanic rock. Associated Press photographer, Joe Rosenthal, had followed this small band of men to the summit. His timely photograph became widely circulated and admired throughout the world. It symbolized undaunted American courage and sacrifice for the cause of freedom.

Working from the original photograph, with the three surviving servicemen posing for him, sculptor Felix de Weldon molded an exact, life-like bronze image of this heroic epic. The entire work of art is upheld by a black granite pedestal, upon which these words are engraved in gold lettering:

In Honor and Memory of the Men of the United States Marine Corps who have given their lives in the Service of their Country since 10 November, 1775.

Dedication ceremonies took place on November 10, 1954, commemorating the 179th anniversary of the Marine Corps. Each of the statues is 32 feet tall, the overall monument standing 78 feet in height. The M-1 rifle held by one of the figures is approximately 16 feet long, the carbines 12 feet long, and the cantines attached to their waists have a capacity to hold 32 quarts of water.

On a hill overlooking the nation's capital, the Iwo Jima Memorial holds a timeless message for each American. It recalls in graphic detail, the high price of liberty, and the pride and courage with which our valiant soldiers have defended it for the past 200 years.[9]

The Netherlands Carillon

Overlooking our nation's capital, adjacent to the Marine Corps Memorial grounds, stands the Netherlands Carillon. In the Spring of 1952, Queen Juliana of the Netherlands presented a model of this carillon to the people of the United States. At the time of its dedication, she expressed her gratitude to the United States for its timely help following the devastation of the Second World War:

> The Netherlands people from all strata, have contributed to this gift, and the bells which are to follow come from various groups of the population: seamen, miners, farmers, flower-growers, fishermen, the armed services, teachers and scientists, financiers and shopkeepers, businessmen and drivers, pressmen, artists, women's organizations, sportsmen and civil servants, resistance people who cooperated with your troops, students, boys and girls, and little children. Each of the Dutch provinces wishes that one of the bells shall bear its name as well. The Antilles, the territories in the Caribbean, join in this present. And Surinam too wants to express its gratitude in its own way to the people of the United States.[10]

The world's greatest bell-founders, Pierre and François Hemony, lived in 17th century Holland. Each of the 49 bells in the carillon represents a province of Holland or a segment of Dutch society which donated it. Inscribed messages upon a number of these reflect their faith and trust in the Lord.

The Sixteenth Bell, extolling the Merchant Marine, has this to say: "You who set your course between the stars and the waves pray the Lord for protection and a favorable wind."[11]

The Thirtieth Bell, dedicated to farmers, reads: "They who resolutely sow new seed, will reap a rich harvest with the help of the Lord."[12]

The Thirty-second Bell is dedicated to the Arts. Its joyful statement is that — "The breath of God is in their work and shows us, how they create for us out of nothing."[13]

Chapter 12

Twelfth Tour:
The Last Tour

The Taft Memorial • The Bureau of Engraving and
Printing • Martha Washington's Bible

The Taft Memorial

An 11-foot bronze statue of Senator Robert A. Taft, son of
past President and Supreme Court Justice William Howard
Taft, stands out in quiet strength and beauty on the slope
leading up to the Capitol's predominance. The tall, matchbox-
like carillon behind it towers 100 feet above the figure.
Twenty-seven, beautifully-matched bells mark each hour and
quarter hour as they pass by.

On various occasions each Sunday and at noon each day of
the week, hymns to the honor and glory of God are played,
such as: "Nearer My God to Thee," "O God Our Help in Ages
Past," "Take Time to Be Holy," and "The Star-Spangled Banner."[1] During the week celebrating Christmas each year, carols
ring out their joyous praise for a Messiah. Included in this
repertoire are old-fashioned favorites such as: "O Come
Emmanuel," "O Little Town of Bethlehem," "O Worship the
King," "Silent Night," and "The First Noël." This impressive
memorial was presented by the people of the United States to
Congress.[2]

*(Editor's Note: Since the completion of this chapter, the mag-
nificent music of the Taft Carillon has been silenced, beginning*

163

in the fall of 1986. The Chief Engineer of the Architect of the Capitol's Office, which holds jurisdiction over this carillon, tells the author that there still remains a major problem in terms of faulty equipment which can only be replaced by a Philadelphia firm. From what he said, it was initially turned off last fall due to complaints from the office buildings in the general vicinity of Capitol Hill and will never be played again during the week.)

The Bureau of Engraving and Printing

Located on the west side of 14th Street at C Street, S.W., this facility is a must for all who enjoy stamp collecting and the intricacies of the printing press. 1864 marked the year for a recommendation of the establishment of an Engraving and Printing Bureau of the Treasury Department. Four short years later, with passage of the Appropriation Act of March 3, 1869, "The Engraving and Printing Bureau" came into being. By the year 1877, all U.S. currency, its principal product, was printed in this bureau.

Portraits of three great First Officers of our nation, each of whom exemplified the Christian principles upon which this country was founded, appear upon the $1, $2 and $5 notes. They are: Washington, Jefferson and Lincoln, respectively.

Another important function of the Bureau is the production of postage stamps for the United States Postal Service. Designations, such as the "Americana Series" of 1975; the "Prominent Americans Series" of 1965; the "Liberty Series" of 1954 and the "Presidential Series" of 1938, are often used for these. The function of Memorial stamps is to honour great people of calibre; worthwhile achievements; anniversaries, expositions and historical events of great significance. A self-guided, recorded tour ends in the gift shop towards the rear of the building, where a magnificent and unique NASA photograph, showing two-thirds of planet earth, is on permanent display. It was taken from the moon's surface during the successful Apollo 8 lunar expedition. From this famous image of "Earthrise" came the 1969 six-cent commemorative stamp which carries the first four words of our Bible upon its face — Scripture that was read for the first time from the moon to the earth: "In the beginning God ... (Genesis 1:1)

(Editor's Note: Since the completion of this chapter, unfortunately, the magnificent NASA "Earthrise" photograph, together with its explanation and Scripture has been permanently removed from display.)

Martha Washington's Bible

As we began this book with George Washington, it is altogether appropriate to finish it with Martha Washington, America's first First Lady, and Washington's beloved wife. This great woman is known to have read her family bible each morning in her bedchamber from 5:00 a.m. — 6:00 a.m., before commencing her daily duties and responsibilities as wife, mother and grandmother. Her magnificent leather-bound, autographed family Bible is on permanent display in the Museum at Mount Vernon, which stands a short distance from the Washington plantation home. It is well worth your while to visit the museum and see this visible proof that we are truly a Christian nation whose founding parents (mothers and fathers) established their lives upon biblical values.

Although you may still visit the museum on the grounds of Mount Vernon, since completing "God's Signature over the Nation's Capital," this priceless item of our American Christian heritage has been permanently removed to the archives. The librarian tells me that it definitely needed a rest, having been out there much too long.

Fellow Christians, it is the twelfth hour. We as Americans, bearing the noble title of *one nation under God* must return to our godly foundations and biblical truth lest we incur the judgment of Almighty God upon our land. I believe that the God of our founding fathers was speaking through the Presidential Inaugural Scripture chosen by Ronald Reagan, our fortieth First Officer, when he swore allegiance to the Constitution with the left hand upon the Bible. This took place on January 20, 1981 and 1985 respectively.

The Bible used by the President to take the oath of office belonged to his mother, Nellie Reagan. It is *The New Indexed Bible,* King James Version, published by Dickson Publishing Company in Chicago, Illinois. The Bible was opened during the swearing-in ceremony to II Chronicles 7:14.

IF MY PEOPLE, WHICH ARE CALLED BY MY NAME, SHALL HUMBLE THEMSELVES, AND PRAY, AND SEEK MY FACE, AND TURN FROM THEIR WICKED WAYS; THEN WILL I HEAR FROM HEAVEN AND WILL FORGIVE THEIR SIN, AND WILL HEAL THEIR LAND. (II Chronicles 7:14)

His mother wrote a sonnet inside the front cover of the Bible. It reads as follows:

WHEN I CONSIDER HOW MY LIFE IS SPENT

THE MOST THAT I CAN DO WILL BE TO PROVE
'TIS BY HIS SIDE, EACH DAY, I SEEK TO MOVE.
TO HIGHER, NOBLER THINGS MY MIND IS BENT
THUS GIVING OF MY STRENGTH, WHICH GOD HAS LENT,
I STRIVE SOME NEEDY SOULS UNREST, TO SOOTHE
LEST THEY THE PATHS OF RIGHTEOUSNESS SHALL LOSE.
THROUGH FAULT OF MINE, MY MAKER TO PRESENT
IF I SHOULD FAIL TO SHOW THEM OF THEIR NEEDS
HOW WOULD I HOPE TO MEET HIM FACE TO FACE.
OR GIVE A JUST ACCOUNT OF ALL MY WAYS
IN THOUGHT OF MIND, IN WORD, AND IN EACH DEED
MY LIFE MUST PROVE THE POWER OF HIS GRACE
BY EVERY ACTION THROUGH MY LIVING DAYS.

— Nellie Reagan

Within the Bible Mrs. Reagan wrote these notations:

IF IN SORROW, READ JOHN 14
IF PEOPLE FAIL YOU, READ PS. 27
IF YOU WORRY, READ MATT. 6:19, 37
IF DOWN-CAST READ PS. 34
IF DISCOURAGED, READ ISAIAH 40
IF YOUR FAITH BECOMES WEAK, READ HEB. 11

A THOUGHT FOR TODAY:
YOU CAN BE TOO BIG FOR GOD TO USE
BUT YOU CANNOT BE TOO SMALL

Officially Recorded Presidential Inaugural Scriptures

Chosen by U.S. Presidents when Taking the Oath of Office

Compiled by Catherine Millard

Dedication

To Dr. John Mulholland, a true man of God, who encouraged and undergirded me in my spiritual walk, and whose untiring efforts taught me to stand firmly and squarely upon the inerrant, infallible Word of God.

Addendum

Officially Recorded Presidential Inaugural Scriptures

Chosen by U.S. Presidents when Taking the Oath of Office

George Washington was sworn into office on April 30, 1789. The Bible upon which the first President of the United States swore allegiance to the U.S. Constitution was published in London in 1767 by Mark Baskett. This King James Version of Holy Scripture is handsomely illustrated with biblical scenes. After taking the oath of office, Washington kissed the Bible, which had been opened at random to Genesis, Chapters 49-50, due to haste. The page of the Bible which Washington kissed is indicated by the leaf being turned down.

Verses 22-25c, excerpted from Genesis 49, read as follows:

Joseph is a fruitful bough, even a fruitful bough by a well; whose branches run over the wall: The archers have sorely grieved him and shot at him, and hated him: But his bow abode in strength, and the arms of his hands were made strong by the hands of the mighty God of Jacob; (from thence is the shepherd, the stone of Israel;) Even by the God of thy father, who shall help thee; and by the Almighty, who shall bless thee with blessings of heaven above...

On March 4th, 1865, Abraham Lincoln was sworn into office for a second term as President of the United States. *The New York Times* describes the ceremony as follows:

The oath to protect and maintain the Constitution of the United States was adminis-

171

tered to Mr. Lincoln by Chief Justice Chase, in the presence of thousands, who witnessed the interesting ceremony while standing in mud almost knee-deep. The New York Times, New York, Sunday , March 5, 1865.

In his inagural address which immediately followed the oath-taking, the 16th President of the United States incorporated biblical quotations from Matthew 7:1 and 18:7 respectively:

"...But let us judge not that we not be judged..." and "...Woe unto the world because of its offenses, for it must needs be that offenses come, but woe to that man by whom the offense cometh."

Lincoln's only known inaugural Bible is a King James Version of the Holy Bible, published by the Oxford University Press in London. Written on its flyleaf are the following words:

To Mrs. Sally Carroll from her devoted husband Wm. Thos. Carroll 4 March 1861

Immediately following President Lincoln's death, Andrew Johnson was sworn into office at the Kirkwood Hotel on April 14, 1865. His inaugural Bible is the King James Version, published by C. J. Clay, at the University Press, London.

Inscribed on the front inside board of the Bible are the words:

Andrew Johnson's Inaugural Bible. When oath was taken his hand rested on Chapter 20 and 21 of Proverbs. The King's heart is in the hand of the Lord, as the rivers of water; he turneth it withersoever he will. Every way of a man is right in his own eyes: But the Lord pondereth the hearts. To do justice and judgment is more acceptable to the Lord than sacrifice. Proverbs 21:1-3

Ulysses S. Grant was sworn into office for the second time on March 4, 1873. On the second blank leaf of his Inaugural Bible is inscribed:

To Miss Nellie Grant from D. W. Middleton Clerk Sup. Ct. U.S. used for the administration of the oath, on the Second Inauguration of General U.S. Grant, as President of the United States March 4, 1873

The Bible was opened at the beautiful Messianic prophecy of Isaiah, which reads:

And there shall come forth a rod out of the stem of Jesse, and a Branch shall grow out of his roots: And the Spirit of the Lord shall rest upon Him, the Spirit of wisdom and understanding, the Spirit of counsel and might, the Spirit of knowledge and the fear of the Lord; Isaiah 11:1-2

The General is purported to have been pleased with this coincidence, as he was the son of Jesse. On the 5th of March, 1877, Rutherford B. Hayes was sworn into office as the nineteenth President of the United States. The Bible upon which he took the oath of office was a King James Version, printed in London by George E. Eyre and William Spottiswoode, printers to the Queen's Most Excellent Majesty. A single electoral vote won this difficult election for Hayes. Due to the closeness of the election, Psalm 118:11-13 might have been chosen as the Inaugural Scripture:

They compassed me about; yea, they compassed me about: but in the name of the Lord I will destroy them. They compassed me about like bees; they are quenched as the fire of thorns: for in the name of the Lord I will destroy them. Thou hast thrust sore at me that I might fall: but the Lord helped me. Psalm 118:11-13

Inscribed upon the second front blank leaf are these words:

To Mrs. Hayes with the Compliments of D. W. Middleton Clerk Sup: Court U. S. Used for the administration of the oath on the Inauguration of Rutherford B. Hayes as President of the United States. 5th March 1877.

Below, in pencil is the notation:

See 118 Psalm 11 verse etc.
" Psalm 101.

James A. Garfield swore allegiance to the Constitution of the United States on March 4, 1881. His Inaugural Bible is the King James Version, S.S. Teacher's Edition, printed at the University Press, Oxford.

A Certification on the second front blank leaf reads:

Bible used at the Inauguration of James A. Garfield 20th President of the United States 4th March, A.D. 1881. James H. McKenney Clerk Supreme Court U.S. (L.S.) To Mrs. J. A. Garfield with compliments James H. McKenney.

The left margin holds the following hand-written comment:

See Proberbs XXI.

To the left of Proverbs 21, the following notation appears in the same hand:

"verse 1, chapter 21 kissed by President Garfield when taking oath of office."

The verse referred to reads:

The king's heart is in the hand of the Lord, as rivers of water: He turneth it withersoever he will. Proverbs 21:1

Chester Arthur was sworn into office privately in New York City after the death of President Garfield on September 20, 1881, and a second time in Washington, D.C. on September 22 of the same year. His Inaugural Bible is a King James Version, published by

George E. Eyre and William Spottiswoode of London. A statement by the Clerk of the Supreme Court appears near the front:

Upon this Bible the Chief Justice administered the oath of office to Chester A. Arthur 21st President of the United States. (L.S.) James H. McKenney Clerk of the Supreme Court of the United States.

Psalm 31:1-2, the scripture chosen by the President for his inauguration, is marked in pencil:

In thee, O Lord, do I put my trust; let me never be ashamed: deliver me in thy righteousness. Bow down thine ear to me; deliver me speedily: be thou my strong rock, for a house of defense to save me. Psalm 31:1-2

Grover Cleveland's Inaugural Bible was published by the American Bible Society in 1851. He was the only President to hold office for two non-consecutive terms. In the front of the Bible is inscribed:

S.G. Cleveland from his affectionate mother July, 1852.

On the next page is inscribed:

On this Bible the oath of Office was administered to Grover Cleveland 22nd President of the United States by Hon. Morrison R. Waite, Chief Justice of the United States, March 4, 1885, Test: James H. McKenney (L.S.) Clerk Supreme Court of the United States.

The Bible upon which Cleveland took his oath of office was a small, well-worn Morocco-covered, gilt-edged Bible. It was a gift from the President's mother, when, as a youth, he first left home to seek his fortune.

An interesting article by Alexander R. George entitled "Inaugural Pageant" gives us a vivid description of the first Cleveland Inauguration:

Cheers 'like the roaring of Niagara' greeted President elect Cleveland as he rode from the White House to the Capitol in an open barouche drawn by President Arthur's spanking bays. The presidential carriage was lined with black and white robes. Vice-President elect Hendricks rode in another open barouche, lined with crimson satin and pulled by four white horses, two famous Arabians in the lead.

After taking the oath of office President Cleveland kissed the small, worn Bible his mother had given him as a boy when he left home. Phil Sheridan, still vigorous and ruddy, stood nearby.

The 'cameramen' hurriedly spread black mantles over their machines and 'shot' the scene while hundreds of men and boys looked on from the roof of the Capitol. It was estimated there were 150,000 people massed on the grounds and nearby streets...

G. Hazelton, in his book entitled *The National Capitol* writes:

By the President's special request, it (his Bible) was used for the ceremony. It was opened by the Chief Justice without any intention of selecting a particular place and the place that was kissed by the President was, therefore, the result purely of chance. As the type used in the Bible is small, the lips of the President touched six verses of 112th Psalm, from verse 5 to 10 inclusive..."A good man showeth favor, and lendeth: he will guide his affairs with discretion, Surely he shall not be moved forever; the righteous shall be in everlasting remembrance. He shall not be afraid of evil tidings; his heart is fixed, trusting the Lord. His heart is established; he shall not be afraid, until he sees his desire upon his enemies. He hath dispersed, he hath given to the poor; his righteousness endureth forever; his horn shall be exalted with honor. The wicked shall see it, and be grieved; he shall gnash with his teeth, and melt away; the desire of the wicked shall perish." Psalm 112: 5-10

At his second inauguration in 1893, Cleveland's hand rested upon Psalm 91:12-16:

They shall bear thee up in their hands, lest thou dash thy foot against a stone. Thou shalt tread upon the lion and adder: The young lion and the dragon shalt thou trample under feet. Because he hath set his love upon me, therefore will I deliver him: I will set him on high, because he hath known my name. He shall call upon me, and I will answer him: I will be with him in trouble; I will deliver him, and honor him. With long life will I satisfy him, and show him my salvation. Psalm 91:12-16

Benjamin Harrison was inaugurated into office as President of the United States on March 4, 1889. His inaugural Bible is the S.S. Teacher's Edition of the King James Version published by the Oxford University Press. An official inscription on the first blank leaf of his Bible reads:

I certify that this Bible was used in the administration of the oath of office on the fourth day of March, A.D. 1889, to Benjamin Harrison, the twenty-third President of the United States. Melville W. Fuller James H. McKenney Clerk of the Supreme Court of the United States. To Mrs. Benjamin Harrison with the compliments of the Clerk.

The following lines are from Psalm 121, verses 1-6:

I will lift up mine eyes unto the hills, from whence cometh my help. My help cometh from the Lord, which made heaven and earth. He will not suffer thy foot to be moved: he that keepeth thee will not slumber. Behold, he that keepeth Israel shall neither slumber nor sleep. The Lord is thy keeper: the Lord is thy shade upon thy right hand. The sun shall not smite thee by day, nor the moon by night. (Psalm 121:1-6)

William McKinley was sworn into office on March 4, 1897. Justice Fuller's certification, without the seal, is inscribed upon the first blank leaf of McKinley's first inaugural Bible, as follows:

I certify that this Bible was used by me in admastering the oath of office to William McKinley as President of the United States on the fourth day of March, A.D. 1897. Melville W. Fuller Chief Justice of the United States

The President's choice of Scripture passage is then pencilled in, to read:

II Chronicles 1:10

An article appearing in the *Washington Post* of March 5, 1897, elaborates upon this auspicious event:

Sworn on a Bishop's Bible presented to Mr. M'Kinley on behalf of African Methodist Episcopal Church. Supreme Court usually provides the Book on which President takes oath of office.

II Chronicles 1:10 reads as follows: "Give me now wisdom and knowledge that I may go out and come in before this people, for whom can judge this thy people that is so great?"

This is the verse in the Bible that Mr. McKinley kissed yesterday, when Chief Justice Fuller had administered to him the oath of office. It is the 10th verse of the first chapter of II Chronicles. Clerk McKenny held the sacred book which fell open at this chapter, and when the newly-made President bent forward his lips were directed to this verse, probably the most appropriate in the book.

'It is a much larger Bible than you had four years ago,' remarked Mr. Cleveland, who had stood by to Mr. McKenny. 'Yes,' replied Mr. McKenny, who had carried the large volume about for an hour or so. 'I think it has been growing all that time.' The Bible is an unusually handsome and costly copy of the Testaments, made especially for the occasion in Ohio, and presented to the new President by Bishop Arnett, of Wilberforce College, a colored institution in the Buckeye State, on behalf of the African Methodist Episcopal Church. Its covers are of blue morocco with satin linings, white satin panels and gilt edges. A gold plate in the center will be engraved with the following inscription: William McKinley, President of the United States of America. Inaugurated March 4, 1897.

On March 4, 1901, McKinley swore allegiance to the U.S. Constitution with his left hand upon his second inaugural Bible. Beneath the usual certification by Chief Justice Melville W. Fuller, a pencilled inscription reads:

Proverbs 16: 20 and 21.

This beautiful and appropriate inaugural Scripture, chosen by the President, reads as follows:

He that handleth a matter wisely shall find good: and whoso trusteth in the Lord, happy is he. The wise in heart shall be called prudent: and the sweetness of the lips increaseth learning.

Theodore Roosevelt's second inauguration took place on March 4, 1905. Below Chief Justice Fuller's signature, the President had dedicated this inaugural Bible to his son as follows:

To Theodore Roosevelt, Jr. from his father March 4, 1905.

The Clerk of the Supreme Court jotted down for posterity, James 1: 22-23 as Roosevelt's choice of inaugural scripture:

But be ye doers of the word, and not merely hearers only, deceiving your own selves. For if any be a hearer of the word, and not a doer, he is like unto a man beholding his natural face in a glass:

William Howard Taft was the only U.S. President to later become Chief Justice of the Supreme Court of the United States. Inscribed on the third sheet of his own Bible are these lines:

I, William Howard Taft, do solemnly swear that I will faithfully execute the office of President of the United States, and will, to the best of my ability, preserve, protect and defend the Constitution of the United States. Wm H Taft

I certify that this Bible was used by me in administering the oath of office to William Howard Taft as President of the United States on the 4th day of March, Nineteen hundred and nine. Melville W. Fuller, Chief Justice of the United States (L.S.)

I Kings 3:9-11, marked and dated March 4, 1909, was the passage selected by Taft for his oath of Office:

Give therefore thy servant an understanding heart to judge thy people, that I may discern between good and bad: for who is able to judge this thy so great a people? And the speech pleased the Lord, that Solomon had asked this thing. And God said unto him, because thou hast asked this thing, and hast not asked for thyself long life; neither hast asked riches for thyself, nor hast asked the life of thine enemies; but has asked for thyself understanding to discern judgment;... I Kings 3:9-11

Woodrow Wilson's inaugural Bible was first used in his swearing in as Governor of the State of New Jersey, and is dated 11 January 1911. At his first inauguration, in 1913, the passage of Scripture chosen by Wilson was Psalm 119:43-46:

And take not the word of truth utterly out of my mouth; for I have hoped in thy judgments. So shall I keep thy law continually for ever and ever. And I will walk at liberty: for I seek thy precepts. I will speak of thy testimonies also before Kings, and will not be ashamed.

A Senate document of March 5, 1917 records President Wilson's second oath-taking in graphic detail:

Mrs. Wilson rode at Wilson's side in the parade, both to and from the Capitol, and also sat beside him all the time he stood reviewing the parade. Both Mrs. Wilson and Mrs. Marshall, the wife of the Vice President, rode through the parade with the President and Vice President. The fact that the grand Marshal, Major General Hugh L. Scott, Chief of Staff of the Army, stood beside the President all during the review of the parade was also an innovation. Promptly at 11 o'clock the President and his personal party came from the White House. He stepped into an open landau drawn by two mettlesome bay horses, which champed and pawed the ground fretfully. Beside him sat Mrs. Wilson, and in the same carriage were Senator Lee S. Overman of North Carolina, and Representative William W. Rucker of Missouri, Chairmen, respectively, of the Senate and House Inaugural Committees. With Vice President and Mrs. Marshall rode Senator Hoke Smith of Georgia, and Francis E. Warren of Wyoming, members of the Senate Committee. In the Senate Chamber the President was seated in front of the Vice President's desk, and the committee on arrangements occupied seats on his right and left.

It was found, when the President ended his solemn obligation, that he had kissed the Bible upon this passage. "The Lord is our refuge; a very present help in time of trouble." (Psalm 46:1)

As the Chief Justice came to the conclusion of the oath, which the President repeated after him, very slowly, a few words at a time, the Chief Justice paused for a pronounced period, lowered his voice, and said solemnly: "So help you God."

The President slowly and solemnly repeated:

'So — help — me — God...'

President Warren G. Harding was sworn into office on Washington's inaugural Bible, opened at Micah 6:8:

He hath showed thee, O man, what is good; and what doth the Lord require of thee, but to do justly, and to love mercy, and to walk humbly with thy God? Micah 6:8

Calvin Coolidge's second inauguration took place on March 4, 1925. The Bible he used was a gift from his mother when he was but a boy. The President's wife, Grace Coolidge, jotted down these lines in pencil on a blank sheet near the front of the Bible:

This is the Bible upon which the President's hand rested as he took the oath of office March 4, 1925 at Washington, D.C. G.C.

The Clerk of the Supreme Court listed John 1 as the President's choice of Scripture passage for his swearing in:

In the beginning was the Word, and the Word was with God, and the Word was God. The same was in the beginning with God. All things were made by him; and without him was not any thing made that was made. In him was life; and the life was the light of men. And the light shineth in darkness; and the darkness comprehended it not. There was a man sent from God, whose name was John. The same came for a witness, to bear witness of the Light, that all men through him might believe. He was not that Light, but was sent to bear witness of that Light. That was the true Light, which lighteth every man that cometh into the world. He was in the world, and the world was made by him, and the world knew him not. He came unto his own, and his own received him not. But as many as received him, to them gave he power to become the sons of God, even to them that believe on his name: Which were born, not of blood, nor of the will of the flesh, nor of the will of man, but of God. And the Word was made flesh, and dwelt among us, and we beheld his glory, the glory as of the only begotten of the father, full of grace and truth. John 1:1-14

A front page column in the *New York Times,* dated March 4, 1925, gives interesting insight into the Presidential choice:

Coolidge will kiss Bible he first read: His grandfather's book will be open at the first Chapter of St. John. His aged father arrives. Colonel is calm and silent but does remark that President was quiet, even as a boy.

President Coolidge will kiss the Bible at the first Chapter of St. John when he takes the oath of office tomorrow. The Bible is one that belonged to his grandfather, from which it is said, the President learned to read between four and five years of age. According to a friend, the Coolidges were accustomed to read the Bible daily, and as a child, Mr. Coolidge took to reading it as his first book. It appears that he frequently read it to his grandfather, who died when he was about five years of age. The section which he first read was the first chapter of St. John. It had been announced that Colonel Coolidge, the President's father, would bring the family Bible containing the births and deaths of the Coolidges, for use in the ceremonies tomorrow. This proved to be incorrect, and the Bible which is in the possession of the President is his grandfather's, which his grandfather later gave to the President. It is a book about the size of the Bible-class, Oxford edition. It is not the bulky family Bible of tradition. Colonel Coolidge, who administered the oath to his son under the kerosene lamp in his Vermont home in August, 1923, arrived late this evening to be present at the ceremonies tomorrow. He declined to make any comment on things political and did not seem to be any more aroused over the event than he was when his son established the summer White House at Plymouth. He displays no more emotion than the President, and is the same, silent stamp of sturdy citizen. (New York Times, March 4, 1925.)

No inaugural Bible for Herbert C. Hoover has as yet been found. Of the several Bibles in his possession, an American Standard Version comes with the following inscribed card:

Presented by the International Council of Religious Education representing the Educational Boards of the Protestant Christian Churches of the United States and Canada. March 4, 1929.

Proverbs 29:18 was the choice made by this President as he took the oath of office:

Where there is no vision, the people cast off restraint But he that keepeth the law, happy is he. (Proverbs 29:18) American Standard Version

Franklin D. Roosevelt's Bible, dated 1686, is the oldest of all inaugural Bibles, and the only one written in a modern foreign language. This Biblia Hollandica (Dutch) version of Scripture was used by the President during all four inaugurations. It was opened each time to I Corinthians 13:

If I speak with the tongues of men and of angels but do not have love, I have become a noisy gong or a clanging cymbal. And if I have the gift of prophecy, and know all mysteries and all knowledge; and if I have all faith, so as to remove mountains, but do not have love, I am nothing. And if I give all my possessions to feed the poor, and if I deliver my body to be burned, but do not have love, it profits me nothing. Love is patient, love is kind, and is not jealous; love does not brag and is not arrogant, does not act unbecomingly; it does not seek its own, is not provoked, does not take into account a wrong suffered, does not rejoice in unrighteousness, but rejoices with the truth; bears all things, believes all things, hopes all things, endures all things. Love never fails; but if there are gifts of prophecy, they will be done away; if there are tongues they will cease; if there is knowledge, it will be done away. For we know in part, and we prophesy in part; but when the perfect comes, the partial will be done away. When I was a child, I used to speak as a child, think as a child, reason as a child; when I became a man, I did away with childish things. For now we see in a mirror dimly, but then face to face; now I know in part, but then I shall know fully just as I also have been fully known. But now abide faith, hope, love, these three; but the greatest of these is love. (I Corinthians 13) New American Standard Version

Harry S. Truman's Second Inaugural Bible was presented to him by the citizens of Jackson County, Missouri as a memorial to his mother. One of two volumes, this magnificent Gutenberg facsimile is a Latin Vulgate translation of Scripture, being one of two volumes. Truman has penned in ink, at the bottom of the page containing Exodus 20:

I placed my left hand on this 20th Chapter of Exodus, January 20, 1949 when I took the oath of office.

Exodus 20:1-17 reads as follows:

Then God spoke these words, saying, I am the Lord your God, who brought you out of the land of Egypt, and out of the house of slavery. You shall have no other gods before Me. You shall not make for yourself an idol, or any likeness of what is in heaven above or on the earth beneath or in the water under the earth. You shall not worship them or serve them; for I, the Lord your God, am a jealous God, visiting the iniquity of the fathers on the children, on the third and fourth generations of those who hate Me, but showing lovingkindness to thousands, to those who love Me and keep My commandments. You shall not take the name of the Lord your God in vain, for the Lord will not leave him unpunished who takes His name in vain. Remember the sabbath day, to keep it holy. Six days you shall labor and do all your work, but the seventh day is a sabbath of the Lord your God; in it you shall not do any work, you or your son or your daughter, your male or your female servant or your cattle or your sojourner who stays with you. For in six days the Lord made the heavens and the earth, the sea and all that is in them, and rested on the seventh day; therefore the Lord blessed the sabbath day and made it holy. Honor your father and your mother, that your days may be prolonged in the land which the Lord your God gives you. You shall not murder. You shall not commit adultery. You shall not steal. You shall not bear false witness against your neighbor. You shall not covet your neighbor's house; You shall not covet your neighbor's wife or his male servant or his female servant or his ox or his donkey or anything that belongs to your neighbor. (Exodus 20:1-17 New American Standard Version)

The New York Times elaborates upon this event in its January 20, 1949 issue:

Truman and Barkley Take Oaths in Capitol at Noon Record Inauguration seen. President Truman asserted tonight that his supreme interest was to see the United States assume the world leadership that God has intended. He said that he would try to achieve this goal for the benefit of the people of the whole world and not for the selfish benefit of this or any other country... President Truman announced today that when he takes the oath of office tomorrow, his hand will rest on two Bibles, one opened at the Sermon on the Mount and the other opened at the 10 Commandments. He especially recommended the 10th Commandment for observance in the Capital city.

The Chief Executive, it became known also, has promised to turn his private papers over to his home town of Independence, Mo, for deposit in a Truman Museum to be established there. This was disclosed with the announcement that the facsimile of the Gutenberg Bible to be used tomorrow will be placed in the Independence public library until the museum is established. Reporters and photographers were in a swarm around Mr. Truman's desk while he was being photographed with the holy books when the President gave his little homily on the Commandments. Also present were members of the staff and Frank Rucker, Vice President of the Independence Examiner, a daily newspaper, and Homer Clements, Superintendent of Schools of Mr. Truman's home Jackson County.

Texts make a good program: Mr. Truman turned familiarly to the Sermon on the Mount in his plain, favorite White House Bible, and to Exodus in the Gothic Latin he could not read in the Gutenberg facsimile, a 2-volume treasure altogether about eight inches thick. Yesterday, Charles G. Ross, the President's Secretary, was telling correspondents in confidence about the President's selection of the two Biblical texts. A Chicago newspaperman remarked that they made a mighty good program for a President. Today another reporter told the President about this.

'It is a good program,' replied Mr. Truman with emphasis. 'Especially the 10th Commandment. If you read the 10th it will do you a lot of good, especially in Washington.'

In the White House texts issued today, the 10th Commandment was rendered as follows:

"Thou shalt not covet thy neighbor's house, thou shalt not covet thy neighbor's wife, nor his manservant, nor his ox, nor his ass, nor anything that is thy neighbor's."

Dwight D. Eisenhower was sworn into office on January 21, 1953, on two inaugural Bibles, his own West Point (American Standard Version Bible) and Washington's Inaugural Bible. Eisenhower's Bible contains the following lines:

Presented to Dwight David Eisenhower upon his graduation from USMA, June, 1915

II Chronicles 7:14, Eisenhower's choice of inaugural Scripture for his swearing in, is marked with a blue pencil:

If my people, who are called by my name, shall humble themselves and pray and seek my face, and turn from their wicked ways; then will I hear from heaven, and will forgive their sin, and will heal their land. (II Chronicles 7:14) American Standard Version

George Washington's inaugural Bible was simultaneously opened to Psalm 127 on this occasion:

Except the Lord build the house, they labor in vain that build it: except the Lord keep the city, the watchman waketh but in vain. It is vain for you to rise up early, to sit up late, to eat the bread of sorrows: for so he giveth his beloved sleep. (Psalm 127:1-2)

Eisenhower's second inauguration took place on January 21, 1957. At this time, the President's West Point Bible lay under his hand, his choice being the twelfth verse of the thirty-third Psalm:

Blessed is the nation whose God is Jehovah, The people whom he hath chosen for his own inheritance. (Psalm 33:12)

Richard Milhous Nixon was sworn into office on January 20, 1969. A Washington Post article of the same date gives us these details:

Mrs. Nixon will hold two family Bibles opened to Isaiah 2, verse 4, for her husband's oath-taking. The verse expresses the new President's hope that 'nation will beat their swords into plowshares, and their spears into pruning hooks' that 'nation shall not lift up sword against nation, neither shall they learn war anymore.'

January 20, 1973, marked Richard Nixon's Second Inauguration as first officer of the Executive Branch of our government. A *Washington Evening Star* article, dated January 21, 1973, covered the event as follows:

As he did four years ago, President Nixon spoke the oath with his left hand resting on two Nixon family Bibles, 100 and 145 years old. His wife Pat held them. Each was open to Isaiah 2:4, which speaks of nations that "shall beat their swords into plowshares and their spears into pruning hooks, neither shall they learn war anymore."

Gerald R. Ford was inaugurated as 38th President of the United States on August 9, 1974. Raising his right hand, Mr. Ford rested his left hand on a Bible held by his wife and opened to one of his favorite passages, the 5th and 6th verses of the 3rd Chapter of Proverbs:

"Trust in the Lord with all thine heart; and lean not unto thine own understanding. In all thy ways acknowledge Him and He shall direct thy paths."

Then, in a firm voice, he took the oath of office:

"I, Gerald Ford, do solemnly swear that I will faithfully execute the office of President of the United States and will to the best of my ability preserve, protect and defend the Constitution of the United States."

At his inaugural oath-taking ceremony, which took place on January 20, 1977, James Earl Carter made this observation:

Here before me is the Bible used in the inauguration of our first President in 1789, and I have just taken the Oath of Office on the Bible my mother gave me just a few years ago, opened to a timeless admonition from the ancient prophet Micah:

'He hath showed thee O man, what is good, and what doth the Lord require of thee, but to do justly, and to love mercy, and to walk humble with thy God.' (Micah 6:8)

(Excerpted from a Washington Post article dated January 21, 1977.)

On January 20, 1981 and January 20, 1985, Ronald Reagan, our 40th president, made his pledge of allegiance to the Constitution of the United States with his left hand upon his mother's Bible, the New Indexed Bible, King James Version, having selected her favorite Scripture verse:

If my people, which are called by My name, shall humble themselves, and pray, and seek my face, and turn from their wicked ways; then will I hear from heaven, and will forgive their sin, and will heal their land. (II Chronicles 7:14)

For further information about Christian Heritage Tours, and our four video teaching tapes on the Christian heritage of our nation, write or call: **Christian Heritage Tours, Inc., 6597 Forest Dew Court, Springfield, VA 22152. Telephone: (703) 455-0333**

Footnotes

INTRODUCTION

[1] Hagner, Alexander B. *Street Nomenclature of Washington City.* Washington 1897, p. 4.

[2] Kite, Elizabeth Sarah. *L'Enfant and Washington (1791-1792).* John Hopkins Press, Baltimore, 1929.

[3] Olszewski, George J. *The History of the Mall, Washington, D.C.* U.S. Department of Interior, National Park Service.

CHAPTER 1

[1] The National Geographic Magazine, March 1915. Taft, William Howard. "Washington, Its Beginning, its Growth and its Future."

[2] *Washington National Monument, Washington, D.C. Concise Description — Details in the Construction.* From Annual Reports of Col. Thomas Lincoln Casey, Corps of Engineers, Engineer in Charge. February 21, 1885. (Inscriptions on the four faces of the Aluminum point crowning apex of monument).

[3] Washington National Monument Society. *Inscriptions on Memorial Blocks, Interior walls,* Washington National Monument. p. 330

[4] Ibid. p. 333

[5] Ibid. p. 334

[6] Ibid. pp. 335, 336

[7] *Washington National Monument, Washington, D.C. Concise Description — Details in the Construction.* From Annual Reports of Col. Thomas Casey, Corps of Engineers, Engineer in Charge. February 21, 1885. (Articles deposited in recess in the cornerstone of the Monument on July 4, 1848.)

[8]Documented from the published General Orders of George Washington. Mount Vernon Library, Mount Vernon, VA.

[9]A White House Release (Press Secretary).

CHAPTER 2

[1]Engraved upon the mantel of the State Dining Room, The White House. Conger, Clement E., Curator of the White House. Letter to author. 5/3/84.

[2]Meyers, Earl Schenck. *The White House and the Presidency.* Wonder Books, New York, 1965. p. 10.

[3]Ibid

[4]Documented with the Office of the Architect of the Capitol

[5]Ibid

[6]Published letters of Abigail Adams. (Rare Manuscript Division, Library of Congress of the United States).

[7]Ibid

[8]Documented with the Office of the Architect of the Capitol

[9]Treasury Department, Office of the Secretary, Department Circular No. 54. Washington, April 17, 1905

[10]Department of the Interior. National Park Service Fact Sheet

[11]Ibid

[12]Ibid

[13]*Presidential Inagural Bibles. Catalogue of an Exhibition.* November 17, 1968 through February 23, 1969, the Rare Book Library, Washington Cathedral, Washington, D.C.

[14]Ibid

[15]Ibid

[16]Framed letter displayed in the basement of the Supreme Court (together with other historical items.) Removed since chapter was completed.

[17]The United States Capitol Historical Society. *We the People, the Story of the United States Capitol, its Past and its Promise.* Washington, D.C. 1978. p. 77.

[18]Ibid

[19]Ibid

[20]Ibid p. 76

[21]Documented by the Office of the Architect of the Capitol

[22]Ibid

[23]Ibid

[24]Ibid

[25]The Architect of the Capitol under the direction of the Joint Committee on the Library. *Art in the U.S. Capitol.* U.S.G.P.O. Washington, 1976, p. 199.

[26]Authorized by Senator Mark Hatfield

[27]*The Congressional Record,* November 16, 1981

[28]Ibid, *The Congressional Record,* September 16, 1982

[29]Interview with Richard Halverson, Senate Chaplain. July, 1983.

[30]House Document No. 234. 84th Congress, 1st Session. The Prayer Room in the United States Capitol. U.S.G.P.O. Washington, 1956. p. 7

[31]Ibid

[32]Ibid

[33]Documented by the Office of the Architect of the Capitol.

[34]Statistics on file with the Library of Cogress of the United States
[35]Documented with the Library of Congress of the United States.

CHAPTER 3

[1]*A Great National Monument to Religion* Reprinted from the Boston Evening Transcript. June 30, 1923, p. 4.

[2]Satterlee, Henry Y. *Washington Cathedral and the Working out of an Ideal.* 1907. p. 2

[3]Ibid. p. 3

[4]Ibid. p. 4

[5]*A Great National Monument to Religion.* Reprinted from the Boston Evening Transcript. June 30, 1923, p. 4.

[6]Satterlee, Henry Y. *Washington Cathedral and the Working out of an Ideal.* 1907. p.2.

[7]Ibid.

[8]*A Viewbook of the National Cathedral.* National Cathedral Association. Mount Saint Alban, Washington, D.C.

[9]*A Great National Monument to Religion.* Reprinted from the Boston Evening Transcript, June 30, 1923. p. 4.

[10]Documented with the Office of Public Communications of the National Cathedral (Interview with Nancy S. Montgomery, Historian/Executive Editor. 12/30/84.)

[11]Ibid

[12]Ibid

[13]Ibid

[14]The Meeting of the Archbishop of Canterbury and the Primates of the Anglican Community. (Church Bulletin). Washington Cathedral. 26 April — May 1, 1981.

[15]Montgomery, Nancy S. *Stitches for God.* The Cathedral Church of Saint Peter and Saint Paul. Mount St. Alban, Washington, D.C.

[16]Ibid

[17]Ibid

[18] Ibid

[19]Ibid

[20]Bratenahl, Florence. *A Garden for the Ages.* Washington, D.C. 1928.

CHAPTER 4

[1]Papers, letters and documents obtained from the Metropolitan Memorial Methodist Church Archives.

[2]Ibid

[3]Ibid

[4]Ibid

[5]Documentation obtained from the Archives of the Metropolitan Memorial Methodist Church. Stone, Philip. Interview with author. Chief Historian/Tour Guide, Metropolitan Memorial Methodist Church 3/31/85.

[6]Historical information put out by the Metropolitan African Methodist Episcopal Church

[7]Ibid

[8]Ibid

[9]Ibid

[10]Authorized by Dr. Elson, May, 1985.

[11]Ibid

[12]St. Nicolas Russian Orthodox Church. The National Cathedral for the U.S.A. (Documentation put out by the church; Interview with Henry Sawchuk, President, Board of Trustees, St. Nicolas Russian Orthodox Church. 7/13/83.)
[13]Ibid
[14]Interview with Mr. Koines, Historian, and one of the first members of St. Sophia Greek Orthodox Cathedral. 7/18/83.
[15]Ibid
[16]Ibid
[17]*Symbols of the Faith. An Exhibition celebrating the shared heritage of Judaism, Christianity and Islam.* Organized by the National Committee Islam Centennial Fourteen, in conjunction with the National Geographic Society.
[18]Ibid
[19]Ibid

CHAPTER 5
[1]Records of the Columbia Historical Society. Blair: Lafayette Square p. 154
[2]Ibid
[3]A Tribute prepared by direction of Trustees of St. John's Church Orphanage of Washington, D.C. Sarah Williams Huntington. Beresford Printer, 1918.
[4]Ibid
[5]A Tribute prepared by direction of Trustees of St. John's Church Orphanage of Washington, D. C. Sarah Williams Huntington. Beresford Printer, 1918.
[6]Ibid
[7]Ibid
[8]Documented information provided by Elmar Denman, Historian of the New York Avenue Presbyterian Church.

CHAPTER 6
[1]*Mount Vernon, The Home of George Washington* — a pamphlet put out by the Mount Vernon Ladies' Association of the Union, Mount Vernon, Virginia 22121.
[2]*Mount Vernon, an Illustrated Handbook.* Judd and Detweiller, Inc., for the Mount Vernon Ladies Association of the Union.
[3]Ibid
[4]Ibid
[5]Ibid
[6]Ibid
[7]Ibid
[8]Ibid
[9]Ibid
[10]Ibid
[11]Washington's Last Will. *Shanahan's Guide to Washington and Its Environs.* Wm. M. Wright. 1894.
[12]Ibid
[13]Ibid
[14]Letter from the Mount Vernon Ladies' Association Library. Clark, Ellen McCallister, Chief Librarian, Mount Vernon, Va. 3/21/84.
[15]Ibid

[16]Ibid
[17]Copy of letter from Philadelphia, 1787, to Joseph Rakestraw. Librarian, Mount Vernon, Va.
[18]Ibid
[19]Taken from the original letter, possession of the Mount Vernon Ladies' Association. Librarian, Mount Vernon, Va.
[20]Ibid
[21]Ibid
[22]Photographic and descriptive documentation, Curator, Division of Graphic Arts, National Museum of American History.
[23]Descriptive documentation, Curator, Division of Textiles, National Museum of American History.
[24]Ibid
[25]Ibid
[26]Ibid
[27]Ibid
[28]Ibid
[29]Inspection of collection and interview with Reidar Norby, Curator of the National Philatelic Collection. 12/30/84.

CHAPTER 7
[1]Engraved upon Smithsonian Seal.
[2]The Freer Gallery of Art. *The Whistler Peacock Room.* Publication 4024 Washington, D.C. 1951.
[3]Interview with Craig Korr, Curator 12/16/83 and 4/24/84. Review of entire collection. Documented by letter from Mr. Korr.
[4]Ibid
[5]Ibid
[6]Ibid
[7]Engraved upon a bronze plaque in the main foyer of museum.
[8]Letter from Curator of Museum
[9]Letter from Irwin, James B. 3/21/84
[10]Letter from Pogue, William R., Skylab Astronaut. 3/25/84.
[11]Ibid
[12]Letter from Irwin, James B. 3/21/84.
[13]Letter from Borman, Frank. July, 1984
[14]Letter from Caidin, Martin. 3/17/84
[15]Interview with Paul E. Garber. 2/10/84
[16]Ibid
[17]Ibid
NASM facts and statistics authenticated by Derek Elliott, Curator, Manned Space Flight, NASM 1/26/88
[18]House of Representatives Committee on the Library, National Gallery of Art, February 17, 1937 (HJ Resolution 217) Washington, D.C.
[19]Ibid

CHAPTER 8

[1] *Trustees for Harvard University. Handbook of the Byzantine Collection.* Dumbarton Oaks, Washington, D.C. 1967.
[2] *The Franciscan Monastery — The Holy Land of America.* Published for the Franciscan Monastery — The Holy Land of America. 1985.
[3] Ibid

CHAPTER 9

[1] *John F. Kennedy: Words to Remember.* (With a foreword by Robert F. Kennedy). Hallmark Editions, 1967.
[2] John F. Kennedy Center Act. 88th Congress, 1st Session. House of Representatives, December 17, 1963. Report no. 1050, Accompanying H.J. Res. 871.
[3] Documentation from the John F. Kennedy Center for the Performing Arts Library, Washington, D.C.
[4] Ibid
[5] Ibid
[6] Ibid
[7] Ibid
[8] Upon a Red Cross slogan advertising the Red Cross and its usefulness. (The John F. Kennedy Library in Boston.)
[9] August 15, 1896. (Washington Evening Star)
[10] U.S. Laws, Statutes, etc. 1902-1903 (57th Congress, 2nd Session). Public no. 122.
[11] Olszewski, George J., *The Construction History of Union Station.* Washington, D.C., February, 1970.
[12] Ibid
[13] Ibid
[14] Eliot, Charles William. *Inscriptions over Pavilion, Union Station, Washington, D.C.* (Late President Emeritus, Harvard University)
[15] Ibid
[16] Ibid
[17] VOA Fact Sheet, November 1987.
[18] *The Voice of America. A Brief History and Current Operations.* VOA.
[19] Official Information. Interview with Margaret Jaffee, Public Affairs Specialist/Tourguide, VOA. 5/17/84
[20] Interview with Father Victor Potapov, VOA 12/6/83 and 12/31/87.
[21] Ibid
[22] Ibid
[23] Ibid
[24] News Release, U.S.I.A. "VOA to Broadcast first English Language Thanksgiving Day Service from Historic Boston Church. November, 1983."
[25] VOA/Log. Official documentation
[26] Ibid
[27] *The House of the Americas in Washington, D.C.* (information put out by the Library of the Organization of American States).
[28] *Statues in the Gardens of the Pan American Union Building.* (Library of the O.A.S.)
[29] Ibid

CHAPTER11

[1]October 3, 1863. Proclamation for Thanksgiving by the President of the United States of America. signed by the President, Abraham Lincoln. William A. Seward, Secretary of State.

[2]*In This Temple. A Guidebook to the Lincoln Memorial.* Museum Press, Inc., Washington, D.C. In Cooperation with the Parks and History Association. n.d. pp. 32,33.

[3]Conklin, Edward F. U.S. Office of Public Buildings and Parks. Lincoln Memorial, Washington, D.C. U.S.G.P.O. 1927, p. 40

[4]Ibid p. 45.

[5]Ibid p. 46

[6]Ibid

[7]Ibid

[8]*These facts and statistics have been verified with Thomas Sherlock, Historian of Arlington National Cemetery, May 15, 1984.*

[9]*These facts and statistics have been verified Ben Frank, Senior Historian, Marine Corps Oral History Program. May 17, 1984.*

[10]Queen Juliana of the Netherlands' Dedication speech (on record with the Department of the Interior, National Park Service, Washington, D.C.)

[11] *Inscriptions on the Bells of the Netherlands Carillon.* The Dutch verses by Ben van Eysselsteyn. (Courtesy of Paul Goeldner, Associate Regional Director, U.S. Department of Interior, National Park Service).

[12]Ibid

[13]Ibid

CHAPTER 12

[1]Documented with the Office of the Architect of the Capitol.

[2]Ibid

Epilogue

For those of you who, in reading the pages of this book, have realized the need for a Savior and a new lease on life, please pray this silent prayer with me:

Father in Heaven, I come to you humbly, as a child, accepting your free gift of salvation through your Son Jesus' sacrificial death and atonement for my sins. I now accept Him as my Lord and Savior, and I thank you, Father, for this priceless gift of a Messiah. I now repent and turn my life over to you, Lord Jesus, in order to serve you all the days of my life in Spirit and in Truth. I accept your unconditional forgiveness, Father, in Christ's sacrifice on Calvary's cross, and realize that through your grace and mercy, I am now translated into the Kingdom of Eternal Life, have become your beloved child, and that I am sealed with the Holy Spirit of promise forever; for You tell me that if I confess with my mouth Jesus as Lord, and believe in my heart that God raised Him from the dead, I shall be saved. (Romans 10:9) Lead me, I pray, into all truth through your Holy Word, Lord Jesus. Amen.

Signed:
Date:
Time of rebirth into God's family:

192